GH00569868

CANAL TO LLANGOLLEN

A portrait of the Llangollen Branch
of the Shropshire Union Canal

Thomas Pellow and Paul Bowen

The Landscape Press

First Published 1988
Second Impression 1993

Copyright ©   Thomas Pellow and Paul Bowen

ISBN 0 947849 01 7

Printed by Johnsons of Nantwich Limited

BIBLIOGRAPHY

As well as the wide range of company and government records, maps and journals that have been consulted the following publications were found to be both relevant and useful.

Baxter B. — Stone blocks and iron rails (1966)

Boyd J. I. C. — Narrow gauge railways in mid Wales (1970)

Byford-Jones W. — Vagabonding through the Midlands (1935)

Cubbon T. W. — The Wizard Dee (1933)

Denton J. H. — The Montgomeryshire Canal (1984)

Gibbs Sir A. — The Story of Telford (1935)

Hadfield C. and Skempton A. W. — William Jessop. Engineer (1979)

Hadfield C. — The Canals of the West Midlands (1969)

Paget-Tomlinson E. W. — Canal and River Navigations (1978)

Rolt L. T. C. — Thomas Telford (1958)

Rolt L. T. C. — Landscape with Canals (1984)

de Salis H. — Bradshaw's Canals and River Navigations (1904)

Shropshire Libraries — Shropshire Canals (1980)

Smiles S. — Lives of the Engineers (1862)

Wilson E. A. — The Ellesmere and Llangollen Canal (1975)

Wright I. L. — Canals in Wales (1977)

ACKNOWLEDGEMENTS

The authors and publisher wish to thank the following for the use of illustrations on the pages indicated:

Clwyd County Record Office 6 and 37; W. Collins 62; J. Foster Petrie 34; D. George 40; G. Howell collection 22 and 54; L. R. Jennings 50; Mrs. N. Joyce 31; D. L. McDougall 28; National Railway Museum 43; E. W. Paget-Tomlinson 47 and 53; Shrewsbury Local Studies Library 27; Shropshire Star 64; M. E. Ware 14; The Waterways Museum, Stoke Bruerne 12 and 18.

Much personal help and information has been given to us in the preparation of this book. Our thanks are due to:- Mr. Fred Leese, Mr. Richard Jones and Mr. Len Wilson — former employees of the Shropshire Union Railways and Canal Co; Mr. Bill Collins and Mr. Jack Strange — former employees of the L.M.S.R. and B.W.B.; Mr. Chris Brown and Mr. Dave Carsley of the Ellesmere B.W.B. depot and Mr. Geoff Pickles, Resident Engineer of the B.W.B. Llangollen Canal Reconstruction Project; Mrs. J. Barton and members of the Whitchurch archaeological groups; Mr. Richard Dean; Mr. Hyde of Welsh Frankton; Mr. Tony Hirst and Mr. Ron Middleton of the Boat Museum, Ellesmere Port; Mr. R. A. Jamison of the Waterways Museum, Stoke Bruerne; Mr. E. W. Paget-Tomlinson; Mr. J. Stothert; Mr. I. L. Wright and to the staffs of the Local Studies Library Shrewsbury, of the Cheshire County Libraries, of Manchester Central Reference Library and of the Clwyd Record Offices at Hawarden and Ruthin.

In particular we should like to thank Mr. L. J. Boughey and Dr. E. Shearing for their most generous and expert assistance and Mr. John M. Lloyd for drawing the maps and diagrams with such skill and enthusiasm.

CONTENTS

The front cover painting by Alan Firth shows "Wren", a horse drawn narrow boat of the Shropshire Union Railways and Canal Company fleet, beginning the crossing of Chirk Aqueduct to pass from England into Wales. Ahead lies Chirk Tunnel while to the left stands the Great Western Railway viaduct.

"Wren" — numbered 212 in the Shropshire Union fleet — was registered at Nantwich in January 1879 to carry general goods. Her master at the time was Samuel Boaz.

Narrow boats being loaded with limestone, a horse drawn tramway... and the hills of Wales beyond; a scene showing many characteristic features of the canal in its commercial heyday. The photograph, dating from about 1885, shows the view towards Llangollen as taken on the "water line" just below Bridge 41 close to the site of the Sun Trevor Inn. For over a hundred years this tramway — one of several that served the canal — brought limestone down from Trevor Rocks doing so between about 1797 until the beginning of the twentieth century. The rock could either be tipped directly into boats that waited beneath the chute or — as shown here — was loaded from stockpiles beside the canal. Much Trevor limestone was used for surfacing the towpaths of the Shropshire Union Canal system to which this route to Llangollen once belonged.

I : FROM DREAM TO REALITY

Welsh Frankton is a place of memories and moods. In winter it can be a mournful spot, the small cluster of cottages, farms and ivy clad trees seeming apart and forgotten by the modern world as chill winds ruffle the surface of the empty waterway that runs east-west past this settlement on its journey from England into Wales. But given a warm summer's day and the place can be transformed. The canal then comes alive with the sounds of holidays and cheerful activity in the air. The wake from hire craft and privately owned boats alike mingle into waves that can set moored craft and bankside reeds bobbing. A fisherman will take little notice of the tow-path walkers perhaps turning off the main route to explore the flight of four locks that drop away down the branch to the south. At the head of this flight the wall of a small adjoining brick building — the old check house — carries a plaque. This commemorates the 1987 re-opening of these locks while a nearby milepost proclaims that Newtown lies but 35 miles beyond.

But neither of these views of Frankton Junction provide much insight into the hopes and plans of the canal builders — nor does the present day traffic on the waterway even follow the route that was originally intended. To understand the emergence of what is now known as the Llangollen Canal we must look back nearly two hundred years — to when, in the early 1790s, the country was in the grip of "Canal Mania".

The growing transport requirements of the Industrial Revolution generated an intense interest in canals at a time when railways had not yet appeared and when road conditions were poor. With James Brindley notable among its engineers a cut was made from Worsley to Manchester. From its opening in 1761 it was a huge success carrying the Duke of Bridgewater's coal both cheaply and efficiently. A second canal from Manchester to Runcorn also proved highly profitable and by 1777, five years after Brindley's death, his Grand Trunk and Staffordshire and Worcestershire Canals had linked up the great river navigations of the Severn, Trent and Mersey. Immensely valuable in carrying commodities such as coal, pottery and iron, these waterways were also a financial boon to their promoters and investors who were rewarded both by high dividends and rising share prices. Canals had indeed arrived.

Industrialists saw in these new waterways a means of bringing raw materials to their factories and of carrying finished goods to markets all over England and to the sea for export. Farmers and landowners looked to them to provide easy access to urban markets for their produce whilst also being a supply route for the general merchandise, coal, lime, manure and building materials needed by rural communities.

Brindley's dream of a "Grand Cross" of waterways linking up England's four major navigable rivers did not reach fruition until January 1790 when the Oxford Canal opened and forged a link between the Thames and the industrial

Midlands. Enthusiastic promoters then sought to fill in the gaps between the existing canals and river navigations.

It was against this background that on June 28th, 1791 three men met in the Flintshire village of Overton on Dee. Colonel John Kynaston, M.P. for the County of Salop, William Mostyn Owen, M.P. for Montgomery, and the Reverend John Robert Lloyd of Aston came together to discuss a proposed canal which would join the rivers Mersey and Dee to the Severn. Apart from opening up an important new north-south transport route between the ports of Liverpool and Bristol, by such a canal the promoters had important local considerations in mind which included the development of local agriculture and the servicing of the Wrexham industrial area.

Following these private discussions a public meeting was held on 31st August, 1791 at the Royal Oak Hotel, Ellesmere, where a committee chaired by the Earl of Powis was appointed to investigate a line for the canal. From the very start the project was bedevilled by arguments about the canal's route.

Proponents of an eastern route supported a survey by William Turner of Whitchurch. The proposal was that the new navigation was to branch off the existing Chester Canal and its links with the River Dee seven miles from the city, and then head southwards via Tattenhall, and on to Shrewsbury. From Penley a branch westwards was to serve the industrial area of Ruabon and Llangollen, whilst Whitchurch, Grinshill and Llanymynech were also to be similarly served.

A rival group advocated construction on a more direct but hilly and difficult line to the west of the Dee with branches to Ruabon, Llangollen, Whitchurch and Llanymynech. John Duncombe of Oswestry made an initial survey while William Jessop of Newark, a well known and very experienced canal engineer — who had accepted an invitation to recommend a route for the canal — broadly supported such a western scheme in his report to the Ellesmere Canal Committee in August 1792. But Duncombe's original line was to be altered. From the flat Cheshire plain the canal was to climb over 300 feet by heavy lockage to reach the summit level at Wrexham. A 4,607 yard tunnel was to take the canal under Ruabon while massive low level aqueducts were then to be employed in crossing the Dee and Ceiriog valleys to the south. A majority of the Committee accepted Jessop's proposals — apart from the "great tunnel" which he was asked to reconsider.

The costs of building such a route would be considerable. Subscriptions for this venture were taken on September 10th, 1792. The books were opened at about noon and by sunset nearly a million pounds had been confided to the care of the Committee. So great was the response that the applications for shares had to be scaled down in line with the Canal's capital requirements.

Early in 1793 supporters of the conflicting western and eastern routes united in order to promote a Parliamentary bill for the building of the canal, the defeated eastern group being placated by a clause empowering construction of a link between the Whitchurch Branch and the Chester Canal broadly in line with their original thinking. Jessop, on behalf of the Committee, had answered questions about the route before a House of Lords Committee and on April 30th, 1793 an Act of Parliament was granted.

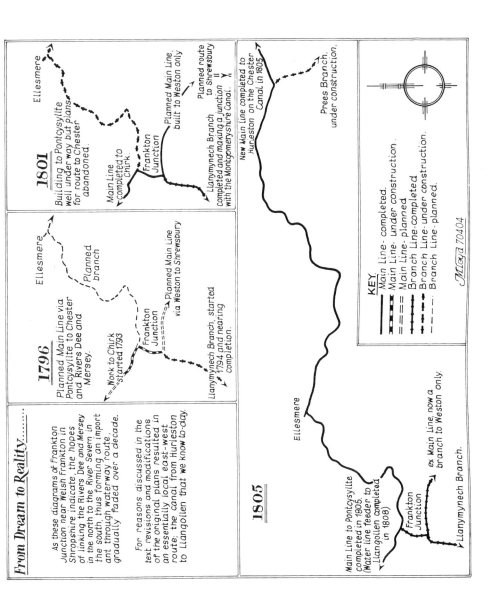

From Dream to Reality......

As these diagrams of Frankton Junction near Welsh Frankton in Shropshire indicate, the hopes of linking the Rivers Dee and Mersey in the north to the River Severn in the south, thus forming an important through waterway route, gradually faded over a decade.

For reasons discussed in the text revisions and modifications of the original plans resulted in an essentially local east-west route, the canal from Hurleston to Llangollen that we know to-day.

1796

Ellesmere

Planned Main Line via Pontcysyllte to Chester and Rivers Dee and Mersey.

Work to Chirk started 1793

Planned branch

Frankton Junction

Planned Main Line via Weston to Shrewsbury.

Llanymynech Branch, started 1794 and nearing completion.

1801

Ellesmere

Building to Pontcysyllte well under way but plans for route to Chester abandoned.

Main Line completed to Chirk.

Frankton Junction

Planned Main Line, built to Weston only

Planned route to Shrewsbury.

Llanymynech Branch completed and making a junction with the Montgomeryshire Canal.

New Main Line completed to Hurleston on the Chester Canal in 1805.

Prees Branch. under construction.

1805

Ellesmere

Main Line to Pontcysyllte completed in 1805.
(Water line feeder to Llangollen completed in 1808)

Frankton Junction

ex Main Line, now a branch to Weston only.

Llanymynech Branch.

KEY
- ▬▬▬ Main Line - completed.
- ═══ Main Line - under construction.
- ╌╌╌ Main Line - planned.
- ┿┿┿ Branch Line - completed.
- ┿┿┿ Branch Line - under construction.
- ╌┼╌ Branch Line - planned.

M.Loyd 70404

Authorised expenditure was set at £400,000 but an additional £100,000 could be called upon if necessary. The auguries were good. Apart from the sound financial start, the Ellesmere Canal was blessed with a strong Committee and an able engineering team. Wealthy landowners such as Sir Richard Hill of Hawkstone contrasted with representatives of the industrial world such as John Wilkinson, the famous ironmaster of Brymbo. The canal's Engineer, the respected William Jessop, was to be assisted by John Duncombe, Thomas Denson and William Turner while in October 1793 a significant appointment was made when the then relatively unknown Thomas Telford became part of the team.

In the north of Cheshire construction of the Wirral Line, the link between Chester and the River Mersey, began in November 1793. Simultaneously work started on the canal's central section from Pontcysyllte south towards Shrewsbury and the River Severn. Work was also started on the Llanymynech branch. The immediate aims were to open up access to the coal mines around Chirk and also to the limestone quarries of Llanymynech. In the Autumn of 1796 eleven miles of this branch were opened south from Frankton to Carreghofa where a junction was made with the Montgomery Canal. The diagram on page 9 shows the position as reached by this time.

In the following year, 1797, traffic began to be carried on the branch while the Ellesmere's planned main line reached Weston Lullingfields where a wharf, four lime kilns, a public house, stables, a clerk's house and a weighing machine were built. The Report to the General Assembly of the Ellesmere Canal Proprietors for 1805 noted that the canal had "promoted the sale of great quantities of lime and slate at Weston Wharf" but despite much debating and surveying the extension south to the River Severn at Shrewsbury was never to be completed. Finance was obviously a major factor but the underlying consideration in the abandonment of its original plan was that the Ellesmere company had been beaten to Shrewsbury. In 1792 a local canal had been promoted to supply that town with coal from the collieries to its east; completed in 1797 a steady coal trade had then begun. So, as the 1805 Report glumly remarked, it was "judged advisable to postpone proceeding further in that direction, because the adjoining country could be supplied with coal and manure from Ketley and Donnington Wood in Shropshire".

The dream of a major north-south canal route linking the Rivers Mersey and Dee with the River Severn thus faded. Although the Wirral Line in the north had been completed and was successfully carrying traffic the original idea of linking this section to the river navigation at Shrewsbury was now seen to be unrealistic. A crucial market to the south had been lost and moreover the central section of the intended main line route was consuming large quantities of finance, energy and optimism.

The navvies were busily engaged north of Frankton where several major engineering works were under construction. The crossing of the River Dee at Pontcysyllte took two years of discussion before in July 1795 William Jessop recommended to the Committee that the canal be carried 125 feet above the river using a cast iron trough supported by masonry piers. The foundation stone was laid on 25th July, 1795 by Richard Myddleton of Chirk Castle who was the local Member of Parliament and also a member of the Ellesmere Canal Committee. Clearly the building of this aqueduct was to be a long term project so in the meantime the Company was keen to generate some income by opening the canal south of Pontcysyllte. Work was therefore concentrated on the much shorter Chirk Aqueduct whose first stone was laid on 17th June 1796. Built at a cost of £20,898, completion came in 1801 but navigation between Frankton and Pontcysyllte was delayed until Chirk and Whitehouses tunnels were finished in 1802. For three years Vroncysyllte Basin became the northern terminus of the Ellesmere Canal.

As for the Ruabon to Chester section there was much talk but little action. The line was resurveyed in 1794 and after acceptance by the Canal Committee on August 10th, 1795, Parliamentary approval for the route was obtained in an Act of 1796. Having dispensed with Jessop's plan for a great tunnel the idea now was that the canal should climb northwards from Pontcysyllte by a flight of locks to reach the short summit level at Ruabon. To overcome the problem of water supply reservoirs were to be built in the narrow valleys of the mountains to the north west of Wrexham. To this end construction of a short feeder canal, known as the Ffrwd Branch near Brymbo, was started in 1796. Although just over 2 miles of this were cut the section remained disused and isolated from the main line.

By 1800 no further progress had been made north of Pontcysyllte and plans for a direct canal to Chester had largely been abandoned. In his report of 24th January, 1800 Jessop wrote that "change of circumstances since the Act have shown it to be wholly inadvisable to execute a canal between Pontcysyllte and Chester, and especially since the extensive opening of the collieries between Hawarden and Flint, which will communicate by railways with the Dee, so as to deliver coal at a much less price at Chester than formerly". Thus for the second time the Company's plans had been overtaken by events; the costly upper end of the planned route to Chester now joined that of the Weston to Shrewsbury section as being an idea that while once offering much could no longer be seen as financially viable. The second diagram on page 9 shows the 1801 position. Already the route was beginning to look but a shadow of the grandiose scheme approved by Parliament some eight years previously.

The conditions created by the Napoleonic Wars had been a major factor. Wartime inflation had pushed up labour and raw material costs, whilst a financial slump at the same time had checked the inflow of funds. The Company's 1805 Report clearly admits that the war years were a difficult time for canal building. "The singular and not unfrequently alarming situation of Public Affairs ever since the commencement of the undertaking, has caused a less rapid progress in some instances, than might otherwise have been made in a time of public tranquility."

As work proceeded at Pontcysyllte, progress was also protracted on the branch being built east of Frankton. In the Ellesmere company's original Act of 1793 powers had been given to construct a link with the unsuccessful Chester Canal to the north east. The beleaguered owners of the latter were no doubt incensed when the Ellesmere's 1796 Bill made no reference to the Chester Canal. Realising that the rejuvenation of their own waterway depended upon a

Pontcysyllte – a contemporary etching of the aqueduct as dedicated to the Ellesmere Canal Company by "their most obedient and humble servant" the artist George Yates of Oswestry. The opening of this masterpiece of civil engineering – the design of which established Thomas Telford at the head of his profession – took place in November 1805, within a few weeks of another national triumph, the Battle of Trafalgar.

physical connection being made with the Ellesmere Canal the Chester Company retaliated by threatening to cease supplying water to the Ellesmere Company's northern section, the Wirral line which had opened in 1795.

The Ellesmere company responded by agreeing to go ahead with constructing a link to the Chester Canal. With the failure of their grander north-south design, this was indeed a logical solution. Had this agreement not been reached then their canal would have been isolated from the remainder of the canal system. Moreover as the Ellesmere company's 1805 Report was quick to point out it "extended the market for coal and lime" and also "carried water for the purposes of the Wirral Line".

By 1797 a link with the Chester Canal had been surveyed. Work on the route east of Frankton began in February of that year but seven years later in 1804 the canal had advanced no further than Tilstock Park, four miles west of Whitchurch. Building had been hampered by difficulties in constructing the Ellesmere Tunnel and also in the crossing of Whixall Moss while Company funds and efforts were really being concentrated on the vast aqueduct works at Chirk and Pontcysyllte. The town of Ellesmere was now served by a quarter mile branch and overlooking the junction a splendid headquarters was built by the canal company which included offices and extensive workshops. Another branch was even begun — cutting south east from Whixall Moss towards Prees — but only the first three and three quarter miles to Quina Brook were ever completed. Nevertheless the Ellesmere Canal Company were optimistic about the branch's future commenting in the 1805 Report that "the adjoining country will be supplied with coal, lime, late, deal and commercial goods and will export oak, timber, grain and cheese".

The 17 miles of canal from Tilstock Park to the junction with the Chester Canal at Hurleston near Nantwich were finally completed in 1805 (as shown in the third diagram on page 9) but this was not the end of canal building for the Ellesmere Company. Their canal had passed to the west of Whitchurch where demand existed for a branch to serve the centre of this market town. In 1808 the navigation opened to Sherryman's Bridge and finally in 1811 to Castle Well where the Earl of Bridgewater, then the Canal Company's chairman, owned land on which wharfage and warehousing were established.

Whilst the Hurleston line was being finished, events were also coming to a climax at Pontcysyllte. Carrying the waterway across the Dee Valley had proved a vast undertaking; apart from the aqueduct itself, the huge earth embankment at the southern end, which was eventually to tower nearly 100 feet above its surroundings, had proved another major task and engineering achievement.

The 26th November, 1805 was a great day for the Ellesmere Canal. At last the aqueduct at Pontcysyllte was to be opened. A reputed crowd of 8,000 thronged the meadows and hillsides and sang 'God Save the King' and 'Rule Britannia' as the first six boats made the crossing. The Canal Committee occupied the first two boats, whilst the third accommodated bandsmen of the Shropshire Volunteers. The canal's engineers and local industrialists crossed in the fourth boat, whilst the last two craft were empty being destined to symbolically load the first coals from the workings at Trevor. A 15 round gun salute by the Royal Artillery Company under the command of Lieutenant Perrott then echoed from the hillside in celebration of a memorable occasion.

North of the aqueduct, at Trevor, a basin had been excavated and a tram road terminated there which served the local collieries and iron-works. With abandonment of the main line to the north this horse-drawn tramroad had been built out of necessity; indeed at one stage, Jessop had even considered permanently terminating the canal at Vron and extending the tramroad across Pontcysyllte.

Despite the canal's brave conquest of the Dee Valley its problems were not over because the question of water supply still loomed. To provide the summit level with water it was decided to build a feeder from Trevor along the northern slopes of the Vale of Llangollen to Llantisilio where water was to be drawn off the Dee at the Horseshoe Falls. An Act of 1804 authorised this feeder but as much of its six miles had to be cut through solid rock the work was not completed until 1808. Although shallow and narrow, it was nevertheless navigable and gave access to the Oernant slate quarries near Valle Crucis and the limestone works at Trevor Rocks.

The completion of this "Water Line" further taxed the Company's financial resources and in July 1806 Thomas Stanton, General Accountant and in effect manager to Ellesmere Company, wrote to principal share-holders requesting £15,000 in loans, "It being necessary for the interest of the Proprietors that the Water Line and other Works now undertaken should be completed as speedily as possible and with more expedition than the present Funds of the Company will admit of".

So by 1806 the Ellesmere Company had spent £459,461 on opening over 70 miles of waterway yet its aim of creating a major trunk route linking the Mersey, Dee and Severn remained unfulfilled. Nevertheless traffic on the Wirral Line to the north was increasing and a viable system of local canals based on Ellesmere had developed which carried a variety of goods such as coal, iron, limestone, lime, slate, timber, granite and grain. Ironically the Ellesmere Canal as built loosely followed the ideas of the supporters of the

The junction of the Whitchurch branch with the main route, circa 1900. This short branch up to the town was the last section of the canal to be built – not being completed until 1811. Though once very busy with cheese traffic it was to close completely after World War II and later to be drained. Lift bridges and fishermen survive however!

eastern route who had been defeated in 1792. Even more ironic is the fact that the canal to Llangollen itself, which now gives its name to the whole waterway, was never intended to be more than a water feeder with a strictly limited commercial potential.

It was a matter of some inconvenience for the Ellesmere Company that the Chester Canal separated the short Wirral Line from the major part of their system. The larger Ellesmere concern made moves to absorb the strategically placed Chester Canal but an early takeover bid in 1804 was to fail. In 1813, however, the two Companies did amalgamate and the 'United Company of Proprietors of the Ellesmere and Chester Canals' came into existence. Under its auspices efforts were directed towards improving profitability; not an easy task in the years of economic recession and social discontent which were an aftermath of the Napoleonic Wars. In their Report of July 1817 the Ellesmere and Chester Canal Committee were "sorry to inform the Proprietors that the same causes which have depressed the general trade and agriculture of the country have considerably affected the Revenue of this Canal. The amount of the Year ending the 30th of June last, being £16,223, whereas the amount of that ending 30th June 1816 was £22,782". Tonnages of lime, limestone, limecoals, firecoals, timber, grain and malt had all fallen sharply and although the Committee "hoped that the trade of the Canal will again considerably improve", a very modest dividend of only £2 per share was declared.

The main handicap for the Ellesmere and Chester, was however, the lack of an outlet southwards to join up with the canals of the West Midlands and thereby the rest of the national system. The Company were no doubt well pleased when, in 1824, news broke of a scheme to build a canal from the old Chester Canal terminus at Nantwich to a junction at Autherley with the Staffordshire and Worcestershire Canal on the northern outskirts of Wolverhampton. The opening of this Birmingham and Liverpool Junction Canal was long delayed until 1835 by which time the threat of railway competition was not far away. To counter this the two canal companies began discussions about a merger and the necessary Act was passed on 8th May, 1845, the new Company retaining the name of the 'Ellesmere and Chester'. A sub-committee was soon set up to consider the future orientation of the Company including the feasibility of converting their canals to railways. A complicated scheme was drawn up involving railway and canal companies, the latter including the Ellesmere and Chester, Montgomery Eastern and Western Branches, the Shrewsbury and Shropshire Canals. Much canal mileage was to be the subject of railway conversion and there were also ambitious plans for new railway schemes. In 1846, therefore, the canal to Llangollen became part of the 'Shropshire Union Railways and Canal Company' but the independence of this new Company was short lived for the powerful London and North Western Railway felt threatened by its ambitious designs. The Shropshire Union directors accepted a financially attractive leasing arrangement and in 1847 the L.N.W.R. assumed control.

This arrangement did not really harm the Llangollen Canal (or as it was then more properly known, the Ellesmere Branch of the Shropshire Union system) for the Committee of Shropshire Union and L.N.W.R. representatives adopted a progressive attitude towards the management of their canals. By the mid-nineteenth century the Llangollen Canal's history had reached a high point but the opening of the Shrewsbury to Chester Railway in 1848 emphasised that the transport industry was changing fast. It was railway competition in the 1850s and 1860s which brought about a sharp decline in the fortunes of this waterway to Wales while road competition in the 1930s was finally to bring its commercial carrying days to an end.

II : BUILDING THE CANAL

Few who cruise the canal to Llangollen will be able to resist turning up the short arm to Ellesmere. Having tied up in sight of the old warehouses that still bear the painted legend "Shropshire Union Railways and Canal Company. General Carriers to Chester, Liverpool, North and South Staffordshire and North Wales" upon their brickwork, they will then wander up Wharf Road to explore the rest of the town. Unassuming and unflustered, with a self-possessed air of rural calm, this little market town of winding streets, tall brick houses and old terraces gives little indication of the excitement it witnessed on 10th September, 1792.

The story of the canal's construction inevitably centres upon the locks and aqueducts, tunnels and cuttings, but before the route could even be pegged out much preparatory work was required, notably in the financial and legal spheres. The potential of a canal linking the waters of the Mersey, Dee and Severn generated enormous enthusiasm with speculators flooding in to seek shares in the scheme from as far away as the East and West Midlands as well as from the surrounding district. "So great is the Navigation Mania" reported the *Chester Courant* that nearby Shrewsbury was so crowded at the time of the subscription meeting that "people found very great difficulty in getting accommodated: several gentlemen being obliged to take care of their own horses, cook their own victuals and sleep two and three in a bed". And to emphasise the extent of the mania it went on to tell how "so difficult was it to procure horses and carriages from Leicester and Market Harborough (on account of the people going from those towns) that six gentlemen from the latter place actually hired and went in a mourning coach". For those who managed to get to Ellesmere by their own means it is reported that they were charged a half a crown (the equivalent to £5 at today's prices) merely to tie their horses to a fence.

Nearly a million pounds were promised that day of which the project had consumed about half by December 1805, mostly derived from the share capital authorised under the 1793 Act. But by this time the inflation of the Napoleonic War period, attractive competing opportunities for investment in government stock and the physical problems confronting the Ellesmere's engineers all served to dampen enthusiasm for the canal.

When in that same year, with a flourish of outward optimism, the first boats crossed Pontcysyllte the Company's fortunes were in truth at a low ebb. No dividends had been paid, plans for a trunk waterway had been replaced by a more local scheme, whilst the vital waterline to Llangollen still remained unfinished. It was within this context that in 1806 the Company approached its principal shareholders — such as Simon Yorke of Erddig House near Wrexham — to request yet further funds which after four years would either be repaid at 5% interest or converted into shares.

BYE LAWS

OF

The Ellesmere and Chester Canal Navigation,

For Regulating the Mooring of Boats on the said Canal during Nights.

JULY 29th, 1841.

No Boatman to be permitted to moor his Boat for the Night, on any part or parts of the several lines of Canal undermentioned, namely :—

On the Chirk Line.

On no part between the Vron Basin near Pontcysylte, and the Wharf at Chirk Bank.—Nor between Chirk Bank and Rhoswiel Wharf.—Nor between Rhoswiel Wharf and St. Martins, or John Evans's Bridge.—Nor between St. Martins Bridge and New Martin Locks.

On the Ellesmere Line.

On no part between New Martin Locks and Maestermyn Wharf.—Nor between Maestermyn Wharf and Frankton Locks.—Nor between Frankton Locks and Tetchill Road Bridge.—Nor between Tetchill Road Bridge and Ellesmere Wharf.—Nor between Ellesmere Wharf and Hampton Bank Lime Kiln.—Nor between Hampton Bank Lime Kiln and Tilstock Wharf.—Nor between Tilstock Wharf and Grindley Brook, and Whitchurch.

On the Prees Line.

On no part between the Roving Bridge on the Moss, except on the Wharfs of the several Lime Kilns.

On the Line from Grindley Brook, to the Old Chester Canal.

On no part between Willymoor top Lock and Wrenbury.—Nor between Wrenbury and Harleston Bridge.

On the Queen's Head Line.

On no part between Frankton lower Lock and the Queen's Head Bridge.

On the Weston Line.

On no part except at the Sycamore Tree, Shade Oak, and Weston Lime Kiln.

On the Llanymynech Line.

On no part between Aston upper Lock and Maesbury Marsh.—Nor between Maesbury Marsh and the Gronwen Wharf.

On the Old Chester Canal.

On no part between Nantwich Wharf and Bar Bridge.—Nor between Bar Bridge and Bunbury Locks.—Nor between Bunbury Locks and Beeston Brook.—Nor between Beeston Brook and Moss Lynn's House.—Nor between Moss Lynn's House and Christleton Bridge.—Nor between Christleton Bridge and Chester.—under a Penalty of TEN SHILLINGS.

EXEMPTIONS.

Any Boat loading or discharging at any Wharf, or discharging place between any of the above stations, may moor for the night only at such Wharf or discharging place.

Lime Boats discharging Lime at any place between any of the above Stations, may moor for the night only at such place at which the Cargo of Lime may be discharged.

Thomas Stanton,

General Agent to the said Canal Proprietors.

Canal-Office, Ellesmere;
November 1st, 1841. }

PRINTED BY W. BAUGH, MARKET-PLACE.

Bye Laws governing moorings as issued from the Canal Office, Beech House, Ellesmere by the long serving general agent to the company, Thomas Stanton. In part such regulations were an attempt to cut down on the poaching opportunities of boatmen who were not averse to mooring near estates rich in game!

In its early days the Company was also preoccupied with securing the necessary Acts of Parliament giving compulsory powers of land purchase. The canal's first Act was passed in April 1793 while others were to follow, as plans were revised and new extensions made. Before a proposed Bill could be presented to Parliament the line of the canal had to be surveyed. Davies and Jebb of Oswestry were active in this capacity being paid £3,010 "for making original plans and books of reference, also the subsequent ones, attending Parliament at sundry times, valuing land and damages during the execution of the work, and making plans of the canal as completed, including expenses". Preparing the Bill and later steering it through Parliament required considerable legal skill which was costly. Messrs. Potts and Leeke, 'solicitors and law agents', undertook much of this work claiming large sums including £3,156 as professional charges for attending Parliament and for business done for the Company from April 12th, 1791 to October 29th, 1805. A total exceeding £10,000 was to be spent on the overall legal costs of the canal.

Landowners whose interests were threatened by the waterway were often vociferous in their opposition but once a Bill was passed they were usually adequately compensated, some £40,744 being spent on actual land purchases. An interesting problem confronted the Company in their desire to cut across common land at Wrenbury. In return for the use of this common an investment was made in Government consols and the interest on these was then used in rate relief for the Wrenbury township.

William Jessop was appointed principal engineer of the canal in 1791 at a time when he was one of the most eminent members of his profession. Born at Devonport near Plymouth in 1745, he was apprenticed to the great John Smeaton through whom he gained widespread experience which included fen drainage, harbour works, lighthouses, bridges, water mills, iron works, river and canal navigations. By the mid-1780s Jessop's technical skills and economical engineering were well known and respected and the next two decades witnessed his most creative period; yet sadly he remains relatively unknown today. The loss of the family papers and his personal modesty played their part, whilst Smeaton's lengthy tutelage over Jessop had perhaps stifled his independence for too long. Nevertheless the Company was fortunate to obtain the services of a first-class engineer who was also a sympathetic and caring person. The safety of workmen on Pontcysyllte, for instance, concerned him and in a letter of July 1795 to his then assistant Telford he wrote "In looking forward to the time when we shall be laying the Iron Trough on the piers, I foresee some difficulties that appear to me formidable. In the first place I see the men giddy and terrified in laying stones with such an immense depth underneath them with only a space six feet wide and ten feet long to stand upon."

The early years of the project saw Jessop laying out the line, completing the first working drawings and attending Parliament as chief engineering witness — but his employment with the Company appears to have ended in 1801 and he did not attend the opening of Pontcysyllte. He had made an inspection of the whole canal early in 1800 and it is evident from his report of this that no longer had he any confidence in the scheme. By this time new projects like the West India Docks were attracting Jessop's services, but his early departure must in part at least have been influenced by the increasing ascendancy of Thomas Telford, the Company's new star who eventually was to gain most credit for the canal's construction.

Born in 1757 at Glendinning in the lowlands of Scotland, Telford was the son of a poor shepherd from the lonely valley of Eskdale. At an early age Thomas was apprenticed to a stonemason at nearby Langholm but in 1782 he moved to London finding employment on the building of Somerset House. His career was greatly helped by the patronage of William Pulteney, M.P. for Shrewsbury. After a spell on harbour works at Portsmouth, Telford moved north in 1786 when he was appointed 'Surveyor for the County of Shropshire' in which capacity he became noted for road, bridge and church building. In October 1793 Telford became 'General Agent, Surveyor, Engineer, Architect and overlooker of the Works' for the Ellesmere Canal Company under the oversight of Jessop. Influential committee members, including Pulteney and ironmaster John Wilkinson, promoted his cause against rivals like William Turner and John Duncombe. This new position was a turning point in Telford's career establishing him as a nationally known engineer. Later achievements were to include the Caledonian Canal, St. Katherine's Docks in London and the Menai Suspension Bridge, but he remained loyal to the Ellesmere Canal acting as its consulting engineer for many years.

Telford's job specification was very extensive and included "the drawing, forming and directing the making of bridges, aqueducts, tunnels, locks, buildings, reservoirs, wharfs, and other works". In addition he was to "superintend the cutting, forming and making of the canal, to give instructions for contracts, to attend himself to the execution of all the contracts, to pay contractors, and workmen, and to keep accounts". For these many tasks the salary was initially £500 per annum, out of which he had to pay a clerk, foreman and his own expenses. This was later dropped to £300 when the assistants were placed directly on the Company payroll. Telford could consider himself lucky to be working under William Jessop for as Smiles was to write in *Lives of the Engineers*, "In all matter of masonry work he felt himself master of the necessary details, but having had comparatively small experience of earthwork and none of canal making, he determined to take advice of Mr. William Jessop on that part of the subject."

In 1805 at the grand opening of Pontcysyllte, Telford was acknowledged as the driving force behind the enterprise and William Jessop was largely forgotten. As the Earl of Bridgewater remarked in the 1805 Report, "The Committee think it but justice due to Mr. Telford to state that the works have been planned with great skill and science, and executed with much economy and stability, doing him infinite credit." Ambitious as Telford was, his personality still retained features developed during his Langholm days, one of which was a firm belief in the virtue of independence. This was applied to quite small and mundane matters like mending his own stockings. A lifelong bachelor he would not permit his housekeeper to touch them but at about nine each evening would go upstairs to his own room and there sit mending them with apparent delight until bedtime.

As well as Jessop and Telford other individuals were prominent in the project. John Duncombe of Oswestry was paid £4,402 between 1791 and 1803 for "making surveys, sections, plans, attending Parliament and acting as resident engineer to the Company" while William Turner of Whitchurch, an active proponent of the Eastern route plan, was also involved in surveying as well as in the production of early designs for an aqueduct at Pontcysyllte. However Telford's appointment in 1793 and subsequent dominance obviously annoyed Turner who appears to have left the Company in somewhat acrimonious circumstances. New men, loyal to Telford, joined the canal building team including Matthew Davidson and John Simpson. Davidson was one of Telford's fellow masons from Scotland and as 'Inspector of Works' he had responsibility for the day to day construction. Simpson was a master mason and had come to Telford's attention during the building of Montford Bridge near Shrewsbury. Apart from his work on the two aqueducts, he was also the major contractor for bridges, tunnels and buildings.

Construction of the Wirral and Llanymynech lines was in hand by early 1794 but attention soon came to be focussed on the crossings of the Dee and Ceiriog valleys. The resultant aqueducts at Pontcysyllte and Chirk were superb pieces of engineering but they were very costly and disguise the fact that the Company's grand plan of a major north-south waterway had been abandoned. Controversy surrounds the precise history of the building of Pontcysyllte and its revolutionary use of cast iron. Initially a traditional masonry aqueduct was envisaged with locks carrying the canal up the valley sides. Early plans along these lines were drawn up by William Turner and approved by the Committee in January 1794. In July 1795 however, William Jessop presented new proposals which involved a high level aqueduct consisting of tall stone piers with a light cast-iron trough.

Telford, writing in his autobiography many years later, claimed credit for this new design. The Committee he wrote was "pleased to propose my undertaking this extensive and complicated work". It has been suggested that the new design was influenced by Telford's experiences with the Shrewsbury Canal to which he was appointed chief engineer in 1795. His first task there was to rebuild an aqueduct across the River Tern at Longdon and instead of stone he proposed an iron structure 60 yards long. Although this was not finished until March 1796, it did give him a working knowledge of iron which possibly influenced the designs for Pontcysyllte which were not finalised until 1797. Canal historian Charles Hadfield has argued that Jessop played a more important role in the birth of Pontcysyllte than has been generally recognised. As the canal's chief engineer it was he who put his weight behind the proposals for an iron aqueduct and secured the Committee's support. Moreover, he was but one of several contemporary engineers who showed an awareness of iron's potential. He had an interest in the Butterley ironworks in Derbyshire near to his own home, while his partner Benjamin Outram had experimented with a small iron aqueduct on the Derby Canal in 1796. The evidence regarding Pontcysyllte is conflicting and confusing but whilst Jessop's role has been undervalued, there appears little doubt that Telford played the major part in the design and construction of the aqueduct. When Telford became first

Pick and shovel, barrow runs, horse and manpower – canal construction and maintenance methods changed little over many years. The photograph, believed to have been taken near Bridge 37 west of Whitchurch in the 1920s, shows a major repair being undertaken with equipment that would have been entirely familiar to the original canal builders.

president of the Institute of Civil Engineeers in 1818, his portrait was significantly painted against its background. In the Scotsman's own mind at least, the aqueduct was largely his personal creation and a major landmark in a distinguished career.

While the first stone of Pontcysyllte had been laid on July 25th, 1795 little further work was done for several years whilst resources were concentrated in the Ceiriog valley to the south. As eventually built the Pontcysyllte aqueduct is 1007 feet long and carries the waterway 127 feet above the river. The nineteen piers are solid for the first seventy feet but to save weight were given two foot thick outer walls and are hollow apart from inside cross walls. At the top they support a cast iron trough 11 feet 10 inches wide. Iron supports in its bed carry a tow path of 4 feet 8 inches, leaving a width of 7 feet 2 inches for boats. The final cost was £47,018. James Varley of Colne was initially engaged to provide stonework but John Simpson joined him in September 1795 and they worked in partnership until the former left in 1800. A very high standard of workmanship was maintained during construction with each stone being exposed to inspection whilst Telford and his foreman Matthew Davidson carefully scrutinized the work. It is reputed that mortar containing bullock's blood was used for extra strength.

William Hazledine provided the ironwork at a cost of £17,284 and this was locally cast at his Plas Kynaston works near Trevor. Iron plates were bolted together to form the trough for the canal and the joints were rendered with Welsh flannel which had been soaked in syrup and boiled. In November 1804 Hazledine was hard at work on his contract, a Company report of the 28th of that month commenting that "the ironwork of the trough part of the Aqueduct of Pontcysyllte over nine arches is now put up". Despite the dangers inherent in the structure's construction only one man lost his life and that owing to his own carelessness. As a contemporary account recorded "he experienced no suffering as the tremendous height from which he fell caused instant dissolution". Almost as much a monument as the aqueduct itself is the large embankment at its southern end. Some 1500 feet long raising this massive earthwork was a considerable feat for local contractor William Davies. Vast quantities of soil were boated from Chirk Cutting to Fron where a light railway was laid to carry the material to the end of the advancing embankment.

Four miles to the south, at Chirk, Telford and Jessop had also opted for a high level aqueduct, the foundation stone of which was laid on June 17th, 1796. Priority was given to its completion before the much more ambitious project at Pontcysyllte in order to provide canal access to the important coal and limestone deposits to the north. Completed in 1801 at a cost of over £20,000 the 700 foot aqueduct is an impressive engineering achievement which towers 70 feet above the River Ceiriog. Piers similar to those later adopted at Pontcysyllte were built but there were important differences. Above the arches three walls ran the full length of the structure and across these the canal's bottom was formed by Hazledine's cast iron plates which were bolted together. Since 1869 the aqueduct has possessed an iron trough — but this was not originally the case. As Telford wrote in his autobiography, "The sides of the canal were made waterproof by ashlar masonry, backed with hard burnt bricks laid in Parker's cement, on the outside of which was rubble stonework." Thanks to the redoubtable John Simpson a first class piece of masonry was produced and Telford a master mason himself, was always in support with practical advice.

When opened in 1801, boats could not navigate north of the aqueduct until the 459 yard Chirk Tunnel had been finished. This, and the much shorter Whitehouses Tunnel, involved gruelling mining through solid rock. Tunnelling commenced at each end but vertical shafts were also sunk for ventilation purposes. Despite the use of gunpowder, much of this work relied upon the brute force of the navvies. At its northern end Chirk Tunnel opens out into three quarters of a mile of deep cutting. Whilst much of the soil was boated away for Pontcysyllte Embankment, there is also evidence of dumping on adjacent land which has resulted in the cutting looking deeper than it actually is. Simpson and Davies, the contractors received £20,554 on this section for "tunnels and deep cuttings by measurement and valuation" but mere financial figures give no insight into the human aspect of canal construction which involved hundreds of men excavating the soil and rock by pick and shovel and then removing the spoil along wheelbarrow runs.

Great as the problems were between the Dee and Ceiriog valleys, the rest of the Ellesmere Canal's mileage still required considerable effort and engineering skill in its construction. The short feeder from Trevor to Llangollen started in 1804, became an expensive undertaking because of the rugged country through which it passed, the 1805 Report commenting on "the considerable quantity of rock that had been cut ... near the upper end at Llandysilio". In all four years of work were needed to complete these six miles.

Further south the section from Frankton to Tilstock also taxed the canal builders, construction lasting a decade from 1797 until 1804. The 1805 Report noted that "this part of the line is carried through a very difficult country and consists of a succession of deep cuttings and embankments, a tunnel near to Ellesmere and two morasses". The latter referred to the peatland known as Whixall Moss where providing suitable foundations took several years. An extensive programme of drainage and dumping was carried out, whilst canal banks were strengthened by the planting of alder trees but the 1805 Report stressed that "although the embankments now appear to be consolidated and firm, a perseverance of strict attention will be necessary for some time". Even the final section to Hurleston was not without its problems for no less than 19 locks were needed and unfortunately several proved difficult and expensive to build because their foundations lay in quicksands.

Cutting the canal inevitably brought inconvenience to some land-owners. Telford in a letter to Davidson, quoted by Gibb in 'The Story of Telford' mentioned that a Dr. Harwood had complained about "Navigators making Havock in his ground". He went on to point out "I should not wish that any unnecessary damage should be done, especially to the Doctor but I strongly suspect that this must arise from the Line being thrown into deep cutting in order to accommodate the Doctor, in which case, I think he should not be so forward and frequent in his complaints". Other landowners were more obliging, Telford citing the example of Mr. Myddelton one of the Company's leading shareholders who showed a "disposition to render the Undertaking much service nor has ever objected altho' the Canal passes near to the first residence in Great Britain, I mean Chirk Castle".

Nevertheless even during the disruptive period of construction, there were positive benefits including stimulation of the local economy in terms of increased demand for labour and raw materials. In the absence of large-scale contractors, the work was distributed amongst several builders including Samuel Betton. He had responsibility for the Frankton to Tilstock section and was paid £39,995 for "works carried on by measurement and valuation" which must have involved the hiring of considerable numbers of navvies. A similar sum was paid to Fletcher and Simpson for the Tilstock to Nantwich section. The procurement of building materials for the canal also assumed importance. Pontcysyllte Aqueduct inevitably consumed great quantities of cut stone and cast iron but even the easier sections of waterway demanded a large volume and wide range of materials. Between Frankton and Tilstock Philip Ireland was paid £324 for timber, Thomas Davies supplied £146 worth of bricks and

£321 was spent on quick-set hedging and trees. Still an interesting feature on this section are the lift bridges, the originals of which were built by a Mr. John Lee at a cost of £234.

By 1808 the Llangollen Canal as we know it had been completed and the once raw earthworks were grassing over and becoming an accepted part of the landscape. As grass and trees colonised the sides of the waterway, the brick and stonework of the bridges mellowed with the passing of the years. Although the Ellesmere Company became preoccupied with promoting traffic on the canal the newly built works could not be neglected as was emphasised in a Report of 1822 by Mr. Joseph Lee and Mr. Exuperius Pickering. On a tour of inspection they noticed that "from New Marton to Chirk Bank the banks, fences and towing paths are in very good repair" but that "the puddle of Chirk Bank still appears to be sinking in places, and to require attention". Moreover, they further discovered that "the towing paths of the tunnels having been formed of timber framings with planking, and gravelled upon the top are decayed and impassable".

It is through careful maintenance that the aqueducts, tunnels, bridges, embankments, cuttings and locks have survived so well into the twentieth century. Compared to more recent engineering feats they might not seem too impressive, but as a product of the 1790s and 1800s they remain a great achievement not only for the famous, like Telford, but also for the thousands of unknown navvies whose imprint on the landscape has been both spectacular and long lasting.

III : CARGO CARRYING DAYS

Watching holiday hire craft negotiating the locks on the Llangollen or cruising a tranquil section of its route it is hard to appreciate how crucial was this waterway to the industrial and agricultural development of the area. Before the cutting of the canal the mineral wealth of the Welsh border country and its rich agricultural potential were isolated, both by distance and poor communication from the growing markets being generated by the industrial revolution. The waterway arose from a demand for better transport facilities in the late 18th century — and for about a hundred and thirty years it was to fulfil the aspirations of its promoters in serving as an effective general cargo carrier. Upon completion there was a natural concern to build up viable levels of traffic, a point emphasised by the Ellesmere Canal report of 1805 in which the Committee announced that "the Navigation is completed for the conveyance of coal, lime and slate in one direction and to the Port of Liverpool and the manufacturing county of Lancashire on the other".

Within a short time a wide variety of goods was bring carried along the waterway, the most important of these being indicated in the canal's Rates of Tonnage published in the Salopian Journal of August 14th, 1816. Specific commodities upon which tolls were charged included limestone, lime coals, burnt lime, fire coals, grain, malt, flour, timber, pig iron, iron ore, bar iron and commercial goods. By 1831 new items had appeared in the Tonnage and Wharfage rates including coke, clay, rock salt, tiles, lead and gravel.

Throughout its carrying history the waterway was busy with agricultural traffic so that with some justification the Llangollen can be described as a 'farmers' canal'. Grain was always an important cargo and in the late nineteenth century much of this was imported through Ellesmere Port and destined for animal feeding. One of the Shropshire Union's major grain using customers were Messrs. A. and A. Peate of Maesbury Hall Mill on the Llanymynech Branch. Former boatmen well remember the days when the waterway was busy with such traffic. Richard Jones, who worked on the route both for the Shropshire Union and later for bye-traders, frequently carried animal feed-stuffs, not only to Maesbury, but also to the Whitchurch warehouse — whilst the Hydes of Frankton operated to Grindley Brook where the filled-in mill arm and corrugated iron warehouse still survive to remind us of this trade. Typical of one of the smaller wharves which handled grain was Platt Lane. There a small brick warehouse with a crane on the side wall once stood by the canal bridge — and older inhabitants of Whixall can still remember the local corn merchant being supplied by boat in the 1920s.

Much of the local grown barley was used for malting. Ellesmere became an important centre of this industry with no less than thirty malt houses in 1861. This perishable commodity was often flyboated to Lancashire for use by the brewing industry but, as with other agricultural products, the levels of this

ELLESMERE & MAESTERFYN
COAL, COKE, & LIME WHARVES
AND
Quina Brook Lime Works, near WEM.

JOHN JONES,
COAL, LIME, & TIMBER
Merchant,

Dealer in every description of English and Foreign Timber, Ladders, Laths, Slates, Hair, Flooring Tiles, Fire Bricks, Fire Clay, Fire Slabs for Grates, Glazed Closet Pans and Traps, Glazed Socket Pipes and Draining Tiles, Grindstones, Plaster of Paris, Portland, Roman, and other Cements, Agricultural and Fine Salt, Artificial Manures, &c.

BOAT BUILDER, COACH BUILDER,
WHEELWRIGHT,
Wharfinger and General Carrier,
CANAL WHARF,
ELLESMERE.

A Large Assortment of
NAVES, SPOKES, AND FELLOES
Dry and Ready for Use, always on hand.
OMNIBUSES, FLYS, CARRIAGES, GIGS, AND POST HORSES ON HIRE AND SALE.
101   N.S.W—VIP

A page from an 1868 trade directory of Shropshire and Wales – making clear how important were coal, lime and timber as cargoes for the canal. The range of other goods as needed by a Victorian agricultural community makes interesting reading. Naves and Felloes are the hubs and rims of wooden wheels respectively.

The Shropshire Union Company's boat "Dora" being reversed into the Ellesmere branch at around the turn of the century. The slotted arm railway style signal probably controlled traffic at this junction in its busier days. A load of timber awaits collection on the tow path, while to the left is the boat-house demolished in the 1950s. Beech House, the original headquarters of the Ellesmere Canal Company, overlooks the scene.

traffic fluctuated, often to the concern of the Canal Company. The Ellesmere and Chester Canal Company Report of 1817, thus referred to the "depressed Agriculture of the County having considerably affected the Revenue of this Canal. In the Articles of Grain and Malt, a great Defalcation has taken place, owing probably to the unfavourableness of the late Harvest and the diminished demand for Malt".

Cheese was another agricultural product carried by boat. Before the First World War frequent cheese fairs took place at Whitchurch and Ellesmere where farmers sold their weekly produce, mainly to Lancashire dealers. Richard Jones also had fond memories of the cheese trade for in the early years of the century he "did nothing else for five years than to take cheese from Whitchurch to Manchester". In the summer time, when plenty of grass would yield much milk for cheese, boats would load at Whitchurch wharf every Saturday. Following a trip via Hurleston, Barbridge, Middlewich, Barnton and Preston Brook, they would then arrive in Manchester on the Monday morning. A peculiarity of the cheese boats was the use of a top cloth painted with white lead — the light colour of which helped reflect the sun's heat away from the hold. Whitchurch's importance in the cheese trade is confirmed by the Shropshire Union's Minutes for October 1891. In the three months to the end of September over 900 tons of cheese were handled. Nearly forty per cent of this originated at Whitchurch, considerably more than from Ellesmere or indeed from elsewhere on the Company's routes.

During its hey-day the canal was also busy with timber traffic. The neighbouring Montgomeryshire Canal, joined via the Llanymynech branch, tapped important areas of woodland while much was also felled locally. References to timber auctions in the 'Salopian Journal' frequently emphasised the value of the Ellesmere Canal as a means of transport for such heavy and bulky cargoes. In the issue for February 4th, 1835 notice was given of an auction to take place at the New Inn, Ellesmere on Tuesday 24th February. "Valuable timber at Brynore, near Ellesmere" was to be sold "consisting of 55 oak trees, 17 ash, 11 sycamores and 1 elm, all within 2 miles of the canal at Ellesmere".

Weston Wharf was active in the timber trade because of the importance of the nearby Boreaton Woods. In 1879 Henry Belcher was using his boat 'The Wellington' to carry the timber from there to his premises at Gnosall in Staffordshire on the Shropshire Union Main Line. The Powis Estate near Welshpool also generated a considerable amount of timber traffic. Richard Jones recalls regular cargoes of oak at the Berriew sawmills before the First World War, while even in the 1920s the narrowboats of the bye-trader J. L. Thomas carried oak from Welshpool to Walsall, there to be used in the manufacture of railway wagons. Hardwood traffic on the canal was mainly outward bound being destined for the industrial markets of the West Midlands and Lancashire; but in the opposite direction there was a busy trade in softwoods from Scandinavia. For example Messrs. R. and J. Tilston who traded at Ellesmere wharf in the 1830s sold such timbers as "Memel, Riga, Dantzig and Pine balk" most of which would have come down the canal from Ellesmere Port.

A multitude of smaller cargoes found their way up and down the canal as building, agricultural and domestic goods came into the district from the manufacturing areas of the West Midlands and from further afield. In exchange cargoes of local produce would return down the canal, many a sack of potatoes being loaded at lock sides and at small local wharves — the farmers concerned both delivering and transhipping their own wares.

By comparison the larger wharves could be quite busy places with several boats unloading at a time and providing valuable employment opportunities for local people. Bagshaw's History, Gazetteer and Directory of Shropshire of 1851, lists four wharfingers at Whitchurch alone. John Brookes and John Humstone worked at Sherryman's Hill Wharf, whilst John Roberts and Thomas Lowe were based at the Victoria and New Canal Wharves respectively. When the waterway came under the aegis of the Shropshire Union official agents for the Company were appointed at important centres both to acquire business and to supervise cargo operations. According to Kelly's Directory of Shropshire for 1885 Thomas Hale was the Shropshire Union agent at Ellesmere while there were similar representatives at Whitchurch, Chirk and Llangollen. The Company's Minutes for June 16th, 1909 suggest that their work could entail a good deal of physical exercise for it was ordered that a "Bicycle be supplied for the use of the Company's Agent at Ellesmere to enable him to visit the customers and wharves in his District, many of which are at a considerable distance from a railway station."

Boatage services on the canal had reached a peak by the mid-nineteenth century. Contemporary trade directories show how well the area was served by the variety of private carriers who worked the waterway through the 1820's and 1830's.

The role of these traders was largely taken over by the Shropshire Union in the late 1840s when its own carrying department was established. For some seventy-five years their boats provided the majority of the services on the canal. Kelly's Directory of 1879 indicates how Ellesmere continued to be the hub of operations. A boat left for Ellesmere Port daily, whilst cargoes to Birmingham were despatched on Tuesdays and Thursdays. Manchester boats left on Monday and Tuesdays, whilst Stoke-on-Trent and the Potteries had the privilege of a daily service. Surely Mr. Charles E. Tisdale, the Shropshire Union agent at Whitchurch was hardly exaggerating when in 1868 he proudly advertised "Boats to all parts of the Kingdom from the Wharf daily!"

Despite the Shropshire Union's own domination of carrying, private operators continued to co-exist particularly in certain trades such as coal and timber. In the 1870s John Jones was one of these bye-traders, owning boats which served his coal, coke and lime wharves at Ellesmere, Wem and Maestermyn. With the dispersal of the Shroppie fleet in 1921, there was a brief resurgence of private carrying before road competition brought the canal to virtual dereliction. As late as 1929 Kelly's Directory of Shropshire was still advertising daily boats from Whitchurch to Ellesmere Port, Birmingham and Stoke-on-Trent, whilst a Manchester boat was scheduled for Saturdays and Cheese Fair Days — but whether these services always ran is very doubtful.

The Llangollen Canal's proximity to mineral deposits such as limestone, granite and slate was also to generate a considerable amount of traffic for the canal. Limestone was the most important of these. Cargoes originated from quarries on the branch at Llanymynech, from Pen y Graig near Fron and from Trevor Rocks on the Llangollen feeder. Much of this was burnt with coal to produce lime in a form which was in great demand by farmers for reducing the acidity and stickiness of the soil, thereby improving plant growth. Significantly the canal's Rates of Tonnage for the early 19th century distinguished between "lime" and "fire" coals, the former being used in limestone burning whilst the latter were of higher quality and used in the home.

Simultaneously with the canal's opening, kilns were built at numerous points along the waterway including a block of six at Froncysylte, three at Hampton Bank, four at Weston Wharf and five at Quina Brook. Narrow boats laden with limestone and coal unloaded their cargoes at these kilns, the tops of which were often level with the canal to facilitate this operation. Burnt lime would then be collected by local farmers but some was also boated to customers. In the 1880s 'Emerald', boat No. 279 in the Shropshire Union fleet, was but one of several involved in this trade between Trevor and Nantwich but by this time the availability of chemical fertilizers was bringing about the closure of many of the lime kilns along the canal.

While limestone contributed to the agricultural development of the area it was also an important industrial raw material. Used as a fluxing agent in the manufacture of iron, huge quantities were boated to the iron making areas of Shropshire and the Black Country. Such boats as 'President' — number 233 in the Shropshire Union fleet and under the command of Joseph Williams — plied between Trevor and Wolverhampton throughout the later years of the nineteenth century. As Fred Leese, another ex Shroppie boatman remembers it was usually a matter of "stones down and mixed goods back". Fluxingstone was also carried to the Humber Arm of the Company's Newport branch, there to be used in the iron industry of the area. This trade reached a peak in the 1860s and 1870s when as much as 15,000 tons per annum were being moved away from the Ruabon area, but by the early 1900's it had all but dis — appeared from the canal due to rail competition. Narrow boats, however, continued to load limestone at Vron Wharf well into the twentieth century, by then such material being in great demand due to the boom in roadmaking.

With slate, limestone, granite and coal to be found along the route of the canal northwards from Chirk — and with yet more limestone to the south along the Llanymynech branch — the canal was well placed to deal with this traffic. But means had to be found to get such heavy and bulky loads to the waiting boats. Before locomotive hauled railways were developed —eventually

Photographs of Shropshire Union boats at work on the Llangollen route are very rare. This postcard – circa 1907 –shows three in the locks at Grindley Brook, bricks apparently being unloaded on the left, perhaps for a repair. While Grindley Brook was provided with proper wharfage the locks on the remoter stretches of the canal were often used as wharves in this way.

The Canal to Llangollen
The route to-day.

The route between Hurleston and Llangollen was
originally known as the Ellesmere Canal with the
branch south of Frankton Junction being its
Llanymynech Branch- at which village it joined
the Montgomeryshire Canal.
  Over the years these original names have lapsed,
those in common use to-day have therefore been
used on this map.

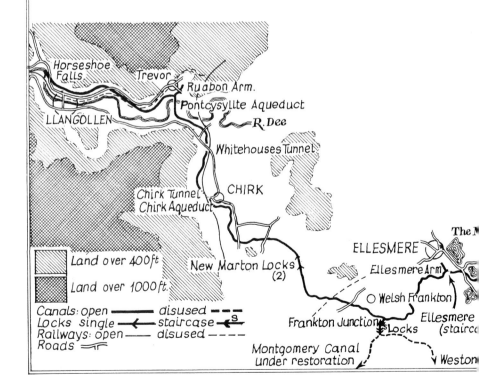

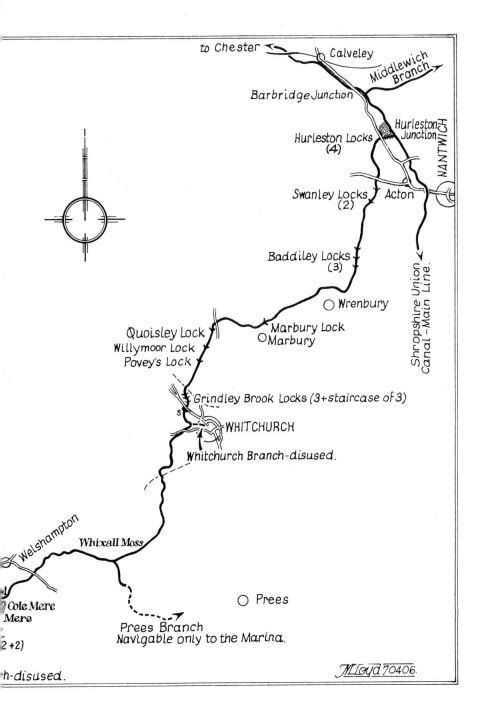

to Chester · Calveley · Middlewich Branch

Barbridge Junction

Hurleston Locks (4) · Hurleston Junction · NANTWICH

Swanley Locks (2) · Acton

Baddiley Locks (3)

○ Wrenbury

Quoisley Lock
Willymoor Lock
Povey's Lock

Marbury Lock
○ Marbury

Grindley Brook Locks (3 + staircase of 3)

S

WHITCHURCH

Whitchurch Branch - disused.

Welshampton · Whixall Moss

○ Prees

○ Cole Mere
Mere

2 +2)

Prees Branch
Navigable only to the Marina.

Shropshire Union
Canal – Main Line.

h - disused.

M.Lloyd 70406.

to take much of such traffic away from the waterway — horse drawn tramways sprang up to transport the stone and coal to the wharves. The Company realised the importance of these rail built feeders and from the start drew attention to their existence. The 1805 Report pointed out that at the (then) northern terminus of the canal at Trevor "an iron railway has been laid ... near Plan Kynaston Stone Quarries, through Acrefair Collieries and is to be continued to the Ruabon Brook". This tramway was eventually to become a standard gauge railway and to be owned by the Great Western — and although canal-rail interchange traffic had died out by the end of the First World War GWR locos would still visit the tracks by the canal basin to fill up with water!

At the northern end of Chirk Cutting the entrance to the Black Park Colliery basin lay off to the right under the bridge –while the narrow gauge lines of the Glyn Valley Tramway reached the canal at this point. Shown here in 1904 the winding hole – ahead and to the left of the moored narrow boat – is all that is left to identify this spot to-day.

Horse drawn tramways of varying gauge ran to the waterway. Slate came down to the feeder west of Llangollen, coal from local collieries was hauled to boats moored at Black Park wharf near Chirk, while limestone bumped down the tracks from Trevor Rocks as well as from the quarries on the Llanymynech branch. But perhaps best known of all the rails serving the Llangollen were those of the Glyn Valley Tramway.

Originally planned to serve the quarries and mills of the valley running down from Glyn Ceiriog towards the Chirk aqueduct the Shropshire Union became heavily involved in the finance and control of the G.V.T. Opened in 1873 the horse drawn wagons had to struggle against a 1 in 24 gradient to reach the canal wharf at Gledrid, and although such traffic was thus diverted from the rival G.W.R. the route ran at a steady loss. After eight expensive years the Shropshire Union decided to withdraw. Backed by the Ceiriog Granite Company — which generated so much of the traffic — the G.V.T. was to go through a period of re-organisation. Steam traction replaced the horses and an easier modified route took the line to exchange sidings at the G.W.R. Chirk station. The tramway still connected with the canal, but now at Black Park wharf. For the next forty six years — between 1888 and 1935 — narrow gauge steam trains rumbled down the Ceiriog valley to provide significant traffic for the G.W.R., but only small amounts for the canal.

Much of the granite transported via the G.V.T. to the canal was in the form of 'setts' — small blocks of stone used to pave the streets of booming towns such as Birmingham and Wolverhampton. By the early twentieth century however there was an increased demand for roadstone and it was in this form that the Shropshire Union boats distributed much of the granite and limestone that they then still carried.

In 1906 the Ceiriog Granite Company installed a new siding, chute and wharf near Black Park Basin to allow narrowboats to load the roadstone more easily. When the Shropshire Union abandoned carrying in 1921 this company also bought some Shroppie boats and even hired some of their ex-boatmen. Richard Jones was one of these and in his regular boat the 'Lord Roberts', was to spend the next decade conveying granite to various wharves for collection by council roadmen. In 1931, however, the Ceiriog Granite Company disposed of their boats as, by then, it was found more economical for lorries to go directly to the quarry. The Hydes of Frankton loaded many a cargo of roadchippings at Black Park wharf. There the Glyn Valley Tramway wagons were tipped, their contents crashing down the chute into the waiting boats. A heavily laden boat was often a problem in Chirk Cutting because of the shallow water there. Sometimes it was necessary to shovel chippings overboard to lighten the vessel but this did little to improve the depth of the water! The Hydes carried the roadstone to many of the scattered wharves on the canal, even on occasions venturing along the now derelict Weston Branch to unload at the almost forgotten Hordley Basin.

Slate was another mineral product to pass down the canal, both from the Ceiriog valley and from above Llangollen. The 1805 Company Report refers to the sale of "great quantities of slate" at Weston Wharf and also the "bringing down of Irenant slate" along the Llangollen water line — but as a volume cargo this failed to fulfil the canal promoters' aspirations. However narrowboats did help supply local communities with roofing slate while some was also shipped further afield. Richard Jones even remembers his grandfather talking of epic trips taking local Welsh slate to London. This was in the 1840s shortly after the opening of the Birmingham and Liverpool Junction Canal. In 1879 'Lydia', Boat No. 274 of the Shropshire Union fleet was still engaged in carrying slates from Chirk to Barbridge Junction but by the early twentieth century clay roofing tiles had started to undermine the demand. T. W. Cubbon in his book *The Wizard Dee* describes coming across a laden slate boat near Llangollen on the eve of the First World War but this must have been one of the last such workings along the canal.

In common with most other waterways coal traffic was always important on the Llangollen. In November 1805, when Pontcysyllte Aqueduct opened, the first boats to load at Trevor Basin had taken on coal from the Ruabon Collieries and the tolls on this cargo were soon a valuable source of revenue. The canal's nineteenth century coal traffic originated in the mines north of Trevor and also those around Chirk. Many local coal merchants were supplied by boat and invariably had canal side premises. Eddowe's Salopian Journal of Wednesday, 5th June, 1816 advertised "coal to be sold from 10d to 11d per cwt. by applying to Messrs. John Bennett and Co. at the New Wharf, Whitchurch". Reference was also made to the "New Wharf Machine" which had been erected by Mr. Hazledine for the Canal Company but which was suspected of underweighing. In tests on 4th June "it was found correct and just" but we are not informed whether the people of Whitchurch were fully convinced!

By the 1860s and 1870s 23,000 tons of coal per annum were being moved by boat from the upper reaches of the canal. By this time there was a declining demand for lime burning coal but nevertheless there were still other canal side industries which relied on water transport for their coal requirements. Both Whitchurch and Ellesmere gasworks remained important customers, whilst as late as the 1920s Peates of Maesbury used the canal to supply their mill with Black Park coal. Bill Collins, who began work on the Llangollen as a lengthsman in 1923, remembers times when two or three boats would visit the Prees Branch each week to unload coal at Dobson's Bridge, while even in the mid-1930s a few locally owned narrowboats, laden with coal, could still be seen plying between the wharves of the Llangollen.

The iron producing area of Ruabon where industrialists like William Hazledine and John Wilkinson were active in the early nineteenth century also benefited from the waterway which transported raw materials and finished products. The Ellesmere and Chester Canal Company's Rates of Tonnage for 1816 refers to "Pig Iron boated from Pontcysyllte to Chester and Iron ore from Chester to Pontcysyllte" all of which were charged at $\frac{1}{2}$d per ton per mile. Bar or wrought iron, which was much in demand by blacksmiths was also distributed by boat from Trevor to various places along the canal.

It is reputed that the Llangollen's most notable cargo of ironwork began its journey at Weston Lullingfields. This consisted of the links which were to form the suspension chains for Telford's Menai Straits Suspension Bridge.

The "water line" from Llantisilio has seen many a load of slate and limestone. This late 19th century scene shows a pair of heavily laden stone boats at White Bridge on the outskirts of Trevor. Bridge, towpath and fencing are all in good condition – characteristic of the Shropshire Union's canals.

William Hazledine was awarded the contract in 1821 and the nine foot long links were made at Upton Magna Forge near Shrewsbury. After testing at Hazledine's Coleham works they were then loaded at Weston Wharf, bound for Chester, from where they were shipped by coaster to the Menai Straits.

The iron industry at the canal's northern end continued to use water transport well into the late nineteenth century. In the 1870s the Plas Kynaston Tube Company was very active and boats departed daily, laden with twenty foot long iron pipes. Further along the canal at Ellesmere the Bridgewater Foundry was located actually alongside the wharf. Not only did it distribute many of its products by water, but also provided ironwork for the Canal Company whose workshops were close by.

The Llangollen Canal also provided safe transport for more dangerous commodities such as chemicals. Most of this traffic originated at Trevor where, in the late nineteenth century, Robert Graesser established a works which, from small beginnings, has today developed into the large and modern Monsanto Chemicals plant. By 1880 half the world's supply of phenol (carbolic acid) originated here while later the derived picric acid, used in the manufacture of high explosive, was to become important. Valuable raw materials like coal tar from the West Midlands came in by boat, whilst refined product such as carbolic acid were shipped outwards.

This chemical traffic persisted into the twentieth century, the narrow boats negotiating the short Pickering's Arm (also known as the Plas Kynaston canal) from Trevor Basin to gain direct access to the works where a crane was used to load the containers. Richard Jones, in his days as a 'Shroppie' boatman, also worked this run and carried oil from there in the early 1900s. During the grim days of the First World War a menacing and unidentified cargo was taken in distinctive white drums to the railway interchange depot at Calveley on the Shropshire Union Main line near Chester. He also vividly remembers the large numbers of women employed at the works during wartime whose clothes were turned yellow by the chemicals used in the factory so that at the end of the day "they looked like canaries walking down the street!"

Even after hostilities had ceased narrow boats still occasionally ventured along Pickering's Arm to the chemical works. In the 1920s the Hydes of Frankton Junction loaded many a cargo of tar there which was then carried to Oldbury in the West Midlands for use in roadmaking. This family carrying firm also supplied chemicals to Richards Bonemeal Works at Rednal on the Llanymynech Branch. But traffic on the canal was becoming a rarity by this time — and during the 1930s it was to completely die away.

IV : LIFE ON THE WELSH CANAL

Like so many boatpeople the majority of those who worked on the Llangollen were born and bred on the canals — and in continuing to work upon them they maintained long family traditions. Richard Jones was born in 1884 at Arddleen on the Montgomeryshire Canal and was to follow both his father and grandfather in working for the Shropshire Union company. Fred Leese, who worked many a stone boat on the Welsh route, had been born near Elworth on the Trent and Mersey Canal — to which he was then to return after his days with the Shroppie fleet had come to an end.

Government censuses emphasise the existence of this tight-knit community, the crews of Llangollen boats almost always having birth places on or near a canal. As 1881 records show, a boat at Grindley Brook was captained by thirty-four year old Enoch Williams who, with his wife, hailed from nearby Whitchurch. Two of their children, Sarah Ellen aged 9 and William aged 5, had been born at Wrenbury also on the Llangollen route, whilst 3 year old John's birthplace was Gnosall, on the Shropshire Union main line. A neighbouring boat moored at Grindley Brook was captained by 46 year old Fred Jones from Welshpool. His wife came from Newtown on the Montgomeryshire Canal while the birthplaces of their three children all had canal pedigrees — Wolverhampton, Newport and St. Martin's.

Family boats were common in the 19th century but it was also practice for captains to hire a mate and leave their wives and children ashore. Thus in 1881 Jane Powell aged 44 was living at Grindley Brook, "her husband" being "with the boat", while at Frankton Locks the census enumerator visited a boat captained by 54 year old Charles Edwards who employed 13 year old Henry Owens as 'servant'. The declining economic viability of canal carrying in the early 20th Century was however to cause a pronounced shift back to family boats as the wife and children provided a free crew.

Life was tough for these people because often the boats would move at first light and carry on for over twelve hours until dusk. There was plenty to occupy the crew; working the tiller, managing the locks, walking with the horse and doing the inevitable domestic chores. Byford-Jones, a Wolverhampton newspaper reporter who cruised the Llangollen in the early 1930s towards the end of its days of commercial carrying, wrote sympathetically about the boatpeople. He was appalled at "the slavery some ... endure" and showed greatest concern for the plight of the younger ones. On lonely stretches of the Llangollen away from the canal officials he found many children hard at work. Their life began at 4 a.m. and often they did not get to bed until late at night. Many young children had little opportunity to attend school and could neither read nor write. Looking after the very young was a particular problem and Byford-Jones saw "one child anchored to a heavy water can on top of the fore cabin, another on the seat in the cabin and tied to the wall to prevent it falling

The 1890s and a gang of lengthsmen at work on the off-side of the canal between Bettisfield and the edge of Whixall Moss. Hedging, ditching, weed cutting and mole catching were all part of the Company's maintenance programme and a large organisation, as was the Shropshire Union, employed many workers in such rural tasks.

off when the boat hit the sides of the lock".

Living conditions on board narrowboats were difficult because normal household tasks such as washing, cooking and sleeping were confined to a very limited space, a fact emphasized by the Nantwich Boat Registry which contains the details of many Llangollen boats. In 1889 the Shropshire Union boat 'Napier' No. 410 operated from Trevor to Nantwich and Wolverhampton carrying stone and lime. The single cabin was 4' 10" high, 8' 0" long and 5' 10" wide yet was registered on the 23rd March of that year as providing living accommodation for two adults and two children. Attempts to regulate conditions on these craft began in the late 19th century with the Canal Boats Acts of 1877 and 1884 which empowered every sanitary authority to report on the conditions of their local boats. Between 1899 and 1904 Edward Green Davies of Gobowen was to produce such reports for Chirk Rural District Council. In 1899 he inspected 25 canal craft. "The condition of the boats" he found "was fairly good and the occupants, being chiefly local residents was satisfactory". Three of the vessels were reported to be in need of painting and one boat's water cask was deemed unsatisfactory. Significantly no infringements of the Canal Boat Acts were noted with respect of cleanliness, ventilation, overcrowding or the separation of the sexes. In 1901 of 14 boats inspected only one was found to be deficient in cleanliness. No legal proceedings were taken as personal warnings sufficed to remedy the situation. Davies was to inspect 13 boats in 1903 but in that year regulations regarding overcrowding, cleanliness and separation of the sexes were all infringed. Looked upon as a whole, however, these reports do not suggest that boats in poor condition were widespread, a point confirmed by people who remember them. According to Mr. Hyde, latterly of Frankton Locks some boats resembled mobile slums but the majority of families took "great care and pride" over the condition of their homes. In his opinion many of the Llangollen boats in the 1920's were 'floating palaces'. The cabins would be decorated with ribbon plates and pictures of roses and castles, brass rings surrounded the chimneys, while the saracen's head of plaited rope at the stern would be scrubbed daily as white as snow.

Boatmens' low pay inevitably meant that they were eager to supplement their income. One method was to obtain free food from canal property or adjacent land. Byford-Jones describes a way. "Every canal boat becomes a trawler on the Welsh branch dragging behind it the line of spoon bait, with which to catch the pike, the large cannibal fish which inhabit these fresh waters. I saw numerous pike, most of them about 2 lb in weight being hauled aboard by barge captains at the tillers of their boats". Fish was a popular and important part of the boatpeoples' diet; surplus was sold off and the money used to buy essentials such as bread, sugar, tea or butter. Large bream, perch, roach, chub and eels also provided tasty meals. The latter were caught by threading small fish onto steel needles which were attached to night lines. The lines were drawn early in the morning "on the ends of them were invariably great fat eels which had completely swallowed the needles".

The towpath and nearby fields were also a profitable source of food. In the warm summer months reported Byford-Jones "men returned from the fields as early as half-past four with great baskets of mushrooms, some for the family breakfast, others for sale". Knowledgeable boatmen would seek out fresh watercress in certain streams, whilst the odd bucket of potatoes or turnips could be lifted discreetly from a farmer's field. Even the shy but attractive moorhen was not safe from predatory boatmen. Skinned and baked with potatoes they provided an attractive supper. Birds eggs were also popular, those of the wild duck being highly prized. In common with most boatmen Fred Leese always kept a dog — in his case a whippet — this being used to catch rabbits in order to supplement the weekly purchase of a joint of meat.

Inevitably the boatpeople's search for self-sufficiency involved a good deal of serious poaching. The proximity of the Llangollen Canal to several important estates provided an abundance of pheasants, woodcock and partridge. Samuel Wildey, master of 'Neptune', admitted that some boatmen hid guns in their cabins for the purposes of poaching. "In lonely parts of the canal they shoot at birds seen in flight and to cover up the sound of gun shots the mate smacks the whip and calls the horse to quicken his pace".

Gamekeepers along the Llangollen always kept a careful watch on passing boats. Near Chirk Castle they were particularly vigilant, frequently walking or cycling the towpath while painted signs warned of the severe penalties for poaching.

Canalside inns provided a rare opportunity for recreation following a long day's work. The Llangollen did not give rise to as many pubs as more heavily used waterways but the names recalled by ex-boatmen from the route include such inns as the Farmer's Arms at Ravensmoor; the Horse and Jockey at Grindley Brook; the Waggoners at Whixall; the New Inn at Gledrid and the Aqueduct at Froncysyllte. Bill Collins of Whixall has fond memories of the Waggoners in the 1920s. Each night a group of boats would be moored at nearby Platt Lane and the horses stabled at the farm by the wharf. The boatmen would be in the pub smoking their clay pipes and he remembers how 'there used to be many arguments there after a pint or two' the noise competing with that of the concertinas and mouth organs providing the music.

Horses and donkeys assumed a position of great importance in the lives of the boatpeople. Shropshire Union boats were entirely horse-drawn until their demise in 1921 while privately owned boats often used pairs of donkeys which were cheaper to buy and maintain. Bill Collins remembers seeing many a pair of donkeys at work in the 1920s and recalls that 'it was surprising how well they pulled the boats along'. Mr. Hyde and family of Frankton kept both horses and donkeys for boat haulage and over the years their animals were involved in several interesting incidents. On one occasion his mother was working a coalboat to Frankton with two donkeys which for no apparent reason suddenly stopped in Ellesmere Tunnel. Having no lantern she used a shovelful of blazing coals from the stove to give some light and soon discovered the reason for the delay. One donkey was pulling towards Ellesmere, whilst the other had turned round and was pulling in the opposite direction!

The use of two donkeys to a boat meant complications with lines and harness, especially at locks and tunnels. Fred Leese recalls his wife being toppled into a lock when sorting out such a tangle — but incidents could also occur with horses. On one trip a Hydes' boat was about to emerge from the northern end of Chirk Tunnel when a southbound boat suddenly entered pulled by a bad tempered horse. The two animals collided on the tunnel towpath while the irate southbound horse kicked out at his boatman! To avoid further incident the Hydes were forced to back their horse to Chirk Basin and to recover their boat afterwards.

Most horses on the Llangollen were well looked after, it being in the boatpeople's own interests to do so. Chopped hay and crushed oats were a common diet for the horses which would often feed from a nose tin as they trod the towpath. The best canal horses were those that went well without persistent driving; these good 'backerers' were well thought of by boatmen who would only need to lead them at locks or towards the end of the day when they tired. Some Shroppie boatmen, however, resorted to cunning to keep their horses moving; many such animals have been encouraged by a clog dangling at its heels from the towing rope!

The relationship between the boatpeople and their horses was often close, ex-Shroppie boatman Richard Jones even remembering the names of some of the animals he worked with seventy years ago. During the First World War when the embankment collapsed at Chirk Bank, his regular horse, "Nelly", was commandeered to pull trucks along a light railway which was laid to take infill from the boats to the breach. Pontcysyllte Aqueduct was sometimes a problem for the horseboats because of its exposed situation. "In rough winds it was not safe to take a horse across and so you'd take him along the road on the Llangollen side and pull the boat across yourself". The metal plates on the aqueduct's towing path were not always to the liking of horses and Richard Jones once had one which refused to cross. Forced to use the whip the reluctant animal moved ten yards forward, jumped into the canal and swam back off the aqueduct! And it was not only animals that caused concern at Pontcysyllte — Fred Leese remembers how many a child had to be locked into the cabin to keep them safe during the crossing.

Apart from the people who lived and worked on the boats, the canal

The Shropshire Union's Committee Boat at Colemere on the 22nd June 1900. While Committee members made regular inspections of the canal the presence of ladies here suggests an outing rather than work. Sixth from the right is George Jebb – identifiable by his white beard and high buttoned jacket. An outstanding Company servant he was its Chief Engineer from 1869 to 1919 and on retirement was retained as "Consulting Engineer".

provided numerous employment opportunities ashore. A valuable insight into the waterway's first generation of employees can be obtained from an 1822 Report by Messrs. Pickering and Lee to the Proprietors of the Ellesmere and Chester Canal. Between Hurleston and Llangollen there were seven lock-keepers and tonnage clerks including Robert Baugh at Frankton Junction and John Furber at New Martin Locks. Each received an annual salary of £39 and also enjoyed use of a company house and garden. Specific responsibility for maintaining sections of the canal lay with seven bank and lock tenders. Mr. John Davies' length stretched from Grindley Brook to Marbury for which he was paid £31. 4s. plus rent free use of a canal cottage. The Company also had several part-time employees; John Roberts was paid £4 per annum for 'Attending the Drawbridge at Tilstock Park', whilst Samuel Moss earned a similar sum for 'locking and unlocking the drawbridge at Wrenbury'.

Most of these men had a long record of employment with the Company indicating a high degree of cohesion and continuity within this community. John Furber had worked on the Ellesmere for sixteen years ever since the opening of Pontcysyllte in 1805, but its longest serving employee at this time was Thomas Telford 'Engineer and general inspector of the works'. The Report records that he received a fee of £100 for his annual inspection and advice but the highest payment went to Thomas Stanton 'Resident Engineer and General Agent' who drew the then very respectable salary of £400.

Government censuses and trade directories also remind us of the wide range of jobs associated with the canal. In the 19th century boat building and repairing took place at several points along the waterway. Pigot's 'Directory of Shropshire' for 1835 refers to Thomas Whittingham 'Boat Builder of Grindley Brook', whilst Slater's 'Royal National Commercial Directory' of 1868 mentions John Jones' business at the Wharf, Ellesmere where 'a great number of hands are now employed at boat and coach building'. According to the 1881 census Job Jones of Dock House, Frankton Junction was the local boat builder, the small repair dock there surviving into the 1930s under the ownership of John Beech who often repaired the boats owned by the Peates of Maesbury Hall Mills.

The Shropshire Union Company undertook most of its own boat building and repair work at Chester but also maintained a much smaller boatyard at Pontcysyllte. Expenses here in December 1872 were but £65 — while at Chester some £769 were reported as having been spent. Canai ticket clerks were also important figures in the daily life of the waterway for to them went the responsible job of assessing the tolls to be paid by each boat. Thomas Shuker held this position at Grindley Brook in 1881 and no doubt he did not envy his colleague Joseph Dudley, a 'canal bank walker' who was out in all weathers doing maintenance and keeping a careful vigil for any leaks. But at least the Shropshire Union seem to have been good employers and to have looked after their staff with a certain charity. In June 1915 the ticket clerk at Frankton —one T. Price — was reported as having been on sick leave with pay since January of that year. As the Company minutes record "he has been found to be suffering from brain affection and will not again be able to resume duty. He is 58 years of age and has been in service 42 years." The Committee agreed that an ex gratia payment of ten shillings per week should be made thereafter, a very reasonable pension for the time.

The Llangollen Canal has produced many notable lock-keepers — often with a considerable record of service. George Howell was one such character. Based at Grindley Brook for many years he saw the passing of the final cargo-carrying boats in the 1930s. When early in the decade Peate's grain carrying boats passed through for the last time the soon to become redundant boatmen were invited into the lock house for a farewell drink. The community which had its origins in the early 1800s and which had bred characters the like of Joe the Snipe, Billy Litteels, Jack the Digger and Maggie the Umbrella was about to disappear from the Welsh Canal.

V : DECAY AND RENEWAL

Unlike most other forms of transport canals readily achieve a unity with the countryside through which they pass — becoming so much part of the landscape that it can be hard to remember that they are indeed man made. Certainly the carrying days on the Ellesmere Canal and its branches reflected this integration with nature. The waterway remains a product of the natural elements of water, wood and stone while the horse drawn boats of mainly wooden construction that once carried their loads of limestone, granite, timber and agricultural products through remote countryside must have seemed artless partners in an arcadian scene.

But the canal had been built for commerce and it was in its links with the industrial Midlands, as well as in serving the needs of a rural community, that it largely fulfilled such a function. By the late 19th century commercial traffic had reached its peak. Thousands of tons of fluxingstone and coal were passing down the canal each year. Regular fly boats ran through to Llangollen and down the Montgomeryshire Canal to Newtown, the horses for these being changed at Frankton Junction. Here at the central crossroads of the Welshward arm of the Shropshire Union system the boat yard, toll office and Canal Tavern all did steady trade while the warehouse was busy with the transhipment of goods. At Whitchurch, Grindley Brook, and elsewhere warehouses also saw regular traffic as did the various coal wharves and lime kilns strung along the route. But the traffic levels of this essentially rural navigation remained adequate rather than outstanding, it being the passage of lime, coal and fluxingstone that sustained the viability of the route.

Company records from the 1870s and 1880s begin to show an element of apologetic humility in the agent's reports on the traffic levels of the Llangollen and Frankton sections. Such cautious phrases as "a fair amount of traffic in the district" and "the loading of boats is up to average" contrasting with the more buoyant and optimistic reports of the agents from the Potteries and other busier areas.

It is clear that the Company viewed the sixty four mile route from Hurleston to Newtown as the main line of the western arm of its system —Shropshire Union distance tables showing the canal from Frankton through Llangollen to Llantisilio merely as a seventeen mile branch. It is also clear that towards the end of the 19th century concerns about the Weston branch were becoming considerable. This six mile section, a sad outcome of the originally planned main line from Chester to Shrewsbury, had become an underused yet troublesome appendage, plagued with leaks and the threat of breaches. With branch profits down to £51 per annum the Company Chairman, Lord Powis, in 1873 had suggested the conversion of the whole Llangollen to Weston section into a narrow gauge railway and the possibility of linking such to the standard gauge railway system at Wem. Nothing came of this proposal,

Pleasure craft have a long history on this canal, particularly at its northern end; horse drawn trip boats on the feeder up from Llangollen dating back to 1884. In the early 1900's the concession for this traffic was held by Captain Jones, here seen at the tiller of his craft — apparently a converted ship's lifeboat.

although gloomy references to lack of profit and maintenance problems continued. A few years later the Company minutes of January 1885 were to record that "the engineer (Mr. George Jebb) brought to the notice of the Committee the condition of the Weston branch canal, the leakage from which was very considerable and suggested the desirability of closing it". He was asked to "consider ways of repairing and protecting the dangerous parts" and "to report again". Two years later similar discussions were extended to include the Montgomeryshire section from Llanymynech to Newtown — while in May 1887 the Executive Committee queried if it was "really advisable to ... keep the (Mongomeryshire) route open to traffic".

The declining fluxingstone traffic from the Trevor area along to Hurleston no longer provided a strong commercial justification for the canal and despite the limited introduction of some pleasure trip boats in the Llangollen and Chirk areas it is evident that by the turn of the century the whole western section of the Shropshire Union system had moved into decline. As if by default the powerful London and North Western Railway Company, which leased the canal, continued to suffer the losses incurred and to ignore the various calls for closure of the more costly and troublesome sections. Their waterway interests were by now largely centred on the Black Country for the busy complex of the Birmingham Canal Navigations was also under their control. As if to emphasise this focus Jebb, who also served as engineer to these navigations, worked from an office at New Street Station, Birmingham. The Welsh sections of the Shropshire Union were thus allowed to continue as a distant and almost forgotten incursion into rival Great Western and Cambrian Railways territory. The legal implications of closure would have been considerable and so, despite physical difficulty and lack of trade, the *status quo* was allowed to continue.

Bradshaw's 'Canals and Navigable Rivers' published in 1904 gives us a contemporary evaluation of the situation on the Shropshire Union at the turn of the century. "There is a fair trade done on the main line of the navigation from Autherley Junction to Ellesmere Port. The general trade on the remainder of the system is not great with the exception of the limestone traffic from Llanymynech on the Ellesmere Canal and from Trevor on the Pontcysyllte branch." It goes on to comment that "the available draught of water ... is somewhat less than that prevailing generally on narrow boat canals but the works are well maintained".

This at least must have pleased Jebb who served the system as chief engineer so loyally and so long — but not so some of the evidence given to the Royal Commission that investigated and reported upon the state of British canals between 1906 and 1911. In his submission to the Commission John A. Harrop, a colliery owner and local politician from Denbighshire, reported that just one small coal mine near Chirk still connected with the canal, the fuel being shipped for local use. He went on to grumble that the canal between Chirk and Llangollen was in such an unsatisfactory condition that "it could only take a 15 to 20 ton load" (i.e. little over half a boat full) while the wharfage facilities perched above the town at Llangollen were "appalling".

In May 1907 Jebb himself was to give evidence to the Commission. He confirmed the small trade in coal and explained that the once considerable trade in limestone for use in the blast furnaces of South Staffordshire now largely went by rail. In answer to Harrop's objections about the "water line" section of the route he pointed out that the canal west of Chirk was not shallow due to neglect but had been built that way. Not surprisingly, in its general evidence to the Commission, the Company stated that in view of the competition from railways, other canals and from bye-traders it could not foresee any great expansion in its traffic in the future.

In 1914 the country went to war. The Shropshire Union, in common with the other railway owned canals, came under the immediate control of the Railway Executive Committee but this was to make little direct difference to the running of the routes to Llangollen, Newtown or their branches. With trade already at a low level they continued to quietly serve essentially local needs. The guns of Flanders and the Somme must have seemed a far cry from the tranquility and rural isolation of such towns as Whitchurch and Ellesmere — but the mosses of Whixall were to see their share of khaki uniforms.

Under the Defence of the Realm Act an army camp was established near Fenn's Bank and work started on building rifle ranges and butts in this area of the moss. To Jebb's concern this was to involve the drainage of adjoining land and he reported to the Executive Committee that "as this may have an injurious effect upon the canal banks the attention of General Busten, who is in charge of the work, has been called to the risks involved". Three rifle ranges were constructed at the eastern end of the moss and a start was made on three more to the west. No doubt Jebb, the professional engineer, smiled behind his neatly trimmed beard when he later reported that "the drainage works have not proved effective and the safety of the canal has not been affected". However the army continued to annoy, for a few months later he was writing tetchily to the Secretary of State for War grumbling about the damage to towpaths being done by troops passing to and from the firing ranges.

But more permanent and telling damage to the canal was to occur in the form of a major breach on the Weston branch in May 1917. In no mood to spend yet more money on an already unprofitable and lightly used branch the Company made no attempt to undertake repairs. Thus the Weston branch became disused, a stub of approximately a mile of navigation remaining between Frankton and Hordley wharf. As if to emphasise that a real run down was now in progress the quarries at Trevor, that for years had supplied the Company with the limestone for towing path surfacing, were abandoned at about this time. The contraction of the system had indeed begun.

During the war years and for some time after Government subsidies had helped the Company cover its continuing losses, but with the ending of such support it was evident that it no longer could continue its business unchanged. In particular the introduction of an eight hour working day and a rise in wage rates made the carrying side of its operation completely uneconomic. The Executive Committee meeting of October 1920 — held at Euston in the principal offices of the LNWR — must have been a gloomy affair, a long discussion as to the advisability of giving up carrying taking place. By 1st June of the following year the inevitable announcement was made. "After much serious consideration" went the wording of the formal notice "it is found impossible to continue ... (the) carrying business under economic conditions" it going on to state that "all Company carrying will stop from August 31st 1921". The announcement concluded with the statement that "the waterway will be maintained in the hope that the public will make use of it on payment of a toll".

Dismantling the considerable undertaking began. The large fleet of boats was put on the market — many of them being sold to local bye-traders. Horses tackle and equipment likewise were sold off. Wherever possible early retirements had been used to cut the labour force while a few of the younger and more fortunate employees were found work with the LNWR. The morale and fortunes of the Shropshire Union were at a low ebb in every sense — even the water supply causing concern. A prolonged drought in the summer prior to the cessation of carrying so depleted Lake Bala as to leave only nine days of water supply available.

It was a subdued Committee that met in October 1921. Carrying had by now ceased and the Chairman opened the meeting with the news that since they had last met it was "with much regret that he had to report they had lost Mr. Whittam, the Company's General Manager since 1912". He had died suddenly in early August, the very last month of carrying and after some thirty-eight years of service with the Company. At the end of 1922 the Shropshire Union was legally absorbed into the LNWR which a few days later, as part of the railway grouping of 1923, was itself absorbed into the new London, Midland and Scottish Railway.

The route of the old Ellesmere canal through to Llangollen and the line to Newtown were to see but little more trade. A short burst of activity followed the abandonment of Shropshire Union Company carrying as the re-organisation of essential traffic took place — but this was to be short lived and was followed by rapid and terminal decline. As well as the sale of boats and horses the infra-structure of the canal trade had been put on the market. The substantial warehousing at Whitchurch was let to the Chester & Liverpool

Whitchurch Wharf in the cold and snow of January 1939. The warehouses and boats, once busy with cheese and other traffic, stand silent – commercial carrying on this once busy branch having finally come to an end.

Lighterage and Warehouse Company who hoped to take over the cheese and other traffic of the branch. For a few years their boats continued the waterborne trade but in 1931 they gave up the unequal struggle of competing with increasingly efficient road transport.

The warehouses at Grindley Brook and Ellesmere were let to local traders and for some years boats of the Fellows Morton and Clayton fleet, who had taken over much of the Shropshire Union carrying trade, worked through to these destinations. The Hyde family of Welsh Frankton continued to carry coal by boat into the 1930s but other long term users of the canal, such as Henry Chesworth's and Son of Nantwich, converted to road haulage even earlier. The Chesworth boat "Burland" was well known on the lower reaches of the canal bringing coal from the Potteries up to Nantwich, Wrenbury and beyond. At one time their Ravensmoor wharf was handling up to forty tons of coal per week but in January 1924 the boat was sold as this company also turned to transport by road.

Perhaps best known of all the bye-traders who had bought boats from the Shropshire Union were A. & A. Peate Limited, the long established milling and animal feeds company based at Maesbury Hall Mill, a few miles south west of Frankton. For many years Canadian wheat had been brought up the canal from Ellesmere Port to their premises. They purchased eleven horse drawn boats from the Company and for a dozen years these plied between the Mersey and Maesbury, each carrying 20 tons of grain inwards, often returning with loads of roadstone from the quarries at Vron. Doing so in order to remain economic they in effect contributed to their own demise. As canal usage and maintenance fell away the waterway slowly silted up so making carrying even harder. Road competition with its higher speeds and markedly lower labour costs became the unavoidable option. In 1934 Peates finally stopped carrying by boat and sold their fleet.

By the mid-thirties commercial traffic on the canal to Llangollen had virtually ceased — only infrequent passages of local slate and coal traffic disturbing the spreading weeds and deepening silt. But the neglect of the canal was to have a more clear cut and dramatic effect on the route from Frankton to Newtown. Nearly a mile down the Llanymynech branch a significant breach occurred on 5th February, 1936. Some forty yards of bank were washed away and a mile of the canal was de-watered. At Welshpool, further south, the sole surviving bye-trader on the Montgomeryshire route, George Beck, was unloading his boat "Perseverance". The breach effectively cut him off from the rest of the canal network as the new owners, the London Midland and Scottish Railway ignored their legal obligations to repair and maintain the route. Beck continued his isolated trade for two more years, eventually being paid £80 in compensation while the railway company sought leave to formally abandon the branch. Meanwhile traffic on the waterway to Llangollen finally died away. The last load between Frankton and Llangollen was of a single ton in 1937 while a final six tons passed between Frankton and Hurleston in 1939. The Montgomeryshire route had been lost and commercial carrying on the rest of the old Ellesmere system was now at an end.

Meanwhile war clouds had once again gathered over Europe and LMS interest in its decaying network of canals to the west of Hurleston was such as to see them as little more than a nuisance value. Legally committed to their maintenance they had already tried unsuccessfully to free themselves of their obligations to the Montgomeryshire route in 1937. An Act of Parliament would now be needed to extinguish existing navigation rights over their extensive network of mainly underused canals across the Midlands and north west England.

With attention diverted by the demands and pressures of war, for five years the western waterways slumbered almost undisturbed. Maintenance gangs continued to work from the Ellesmere depot attending to bank, fence and culvert repairs and mending the inevitable small breaches and leakages — their boats the only traffic on the increasingly weed grown route. But for the occasional glance officialdom took little notice. The closure of a number of LMS canals was briefly considered in 1941 while a year later it was suggested to the railway's Board that the route from Llangollen should be kept open as a feeder if for no other reason than it provided a useful water supply for the steam locomotives shedded at Chester. It was not until 1944 that two Bills were eventually presented to Parliament.

The first of these Bills was to authorise abandonment of over a hundred and fifty miles of LMS owned canals — inclusive of the entire section from Frankton to Newtown and the derelict Weston branch. The whole section now known as the Llangollen Canal — i.e. from Hurleston via Llangollen to Llantisilio — was to be spared so allowing water from the Dee to continue to reach the main line of the Shropshire Union. The second Bill was connected to this reprieve. During the war years the Conservators of the River Dee had discovered that the LMS was selling considerable quantities of water drawn from the canal — this water having been taken from *their* river! The Conservators legally challenged the railway company's right to sell such water, the LMS customers at this time included the Monsanto Chemical Company, whose works overlooked the canal at Pontcysyllte, and the Creamery at Ellesmere. To regularise and protect their position the railway company were obliged to seek a Bill to make this abstraction legal; eventually it was agreed that 6¼ million gallons per day could be metered into the canal from the Horseshoe Falls.

The two inter-related Bills received Royal Assent in December 1944 and thus became law. Under the Abandonment Act responsibility for the road bridges over the canals became the concern of the local highway authorities. To facilitate road traffic a number of bridges on the abandoned Montgomeryshire route were lowered, while suggestions to similarly lower a number of bridges on the Llangollen route were also proposed. Had these proposals been carried out it would have meant that navigation of this waterway would no longer have been possible — but delay followed delay. However when Mr. Christopher Marsh, the Divisional Waterways Officer, was eventually given notice of the lowering of Wenffrwyd Bridge to the east of Llangollen he arranged a meeting with the highway engineers. He argued that there were considerable dredging needs on the stretches to either side of the town. If the highway authorities were to block the canal by lowering this bridge

Following the ending of commercial carrying and before the growth of pleasure traffic the only movement on the canal was that of a few maintenance boats. The horse drawn "Sirius" was one of these, seen here approaching Platt Lane late in the Summer of 1957.

and others they would — under a provision of the closure Act — have to pay the on-going costs of moving maintenance craft around such blockages. The already delayed bridge lowering plans were shelved as the highway authorities re-assessed their position.

The association issue of water abstraction, as defined by the second Act of Parliament, was now to strengthen the case for keeping the navigation open. By the 1950s the expansion of towns and industry in South Cheshire had required that increasing amounts of water were extracted from the Dee and passed down the canal to Hurleston — hence to the taps of Nantwich, Middlewich, Crewe and beyond. Maintenance of the canal, now serving in the role of open pipeline for the water requirements of a large population, emphasised the need for working boats to be able to pass freely along the route. After many representations — from a crusading Inland Waterways Association, a far-seeing Llangollen town council and crucially from the waterways authorities themselves — 1952 saw an agreement reached. At a conference of local authorities it was decided that the bridge approaches

Repairs to Povey's lock in 1948. Due to the poor condition of the canal L.T.C. Rolt had been unable to navigate its length in 1947 although helped through Grindley Brook locks by George Howell — seen here with trilby and rope on the right. When two years later Rolt tackled the canal again he found "the improvements that had taken place ... quite remarkable."

should be improved rather than the bridges themselves being lowered. Navigation was thus to remain possible on the "abandoned" canal.

L.T.C. Rolt's classic book *Narrow Boat* — that was to introduce so many to a love of the waterways — was, like the LMS Bill of Abandonment, published in 1944. The moment was right. Following the rigours of World War II its portrayal of leisured inland cruising combined with a view of an older England found a ready audience — while its concerns for those who still traded on the waterways matched the preservationist aims of the Inland Waterways Association that was to be founded in 1946. The waterways movement was underway and Rolt was in the thick of it. His boat "Cressy" was ex-Shropshire Union and had then become one of the Peate's Maesbury fleet before conversion for cruising. The desire to take her up the Llangollen route, over Telford's magnificent aqueducts at Chirk and Pontcysyllte and so to the boatyard where she had originally been built must have been very strong. And try he did — but was to find the canal in very poor condition when he tackled the journey in 1947. At both Baddiley and Grindley Brook the narrowed lock chambers had to be forced while acres of weed demanded much bow hauling. The voyage was finally abandoned at Ellesmere but two years later Rolt was 'back. Already the canal seemed in better shape, at least in its lower reaches. So in the height of summer Pontcysyllte was reached and "Cressy" made her long delayed crossing of the aqueduct.

Others were to follow and the numbers cruising the canal steadily increased in parallel with the growing national interest and enthusiasm for the waterways. But it was still very difficult to get through to Llangollen. Despite problems with weeds and shallows Edward Wilson, whose enthusiasm for the canal and whose research has provided so much information on its early industrial base and background, made the trip as far as Trevor in 1952. In the same year a rally of twenty-five boats organised by the North West branch of the Inland Waterways Association was held at Llangollen. Slowly the canal was coming back to life.

British Transport Waterways (the fore-runners of the British Waterways Board) were beginning to tackle the immense backlog of maintenance work. Lock gates were gradually replaced, lift bridges repaired and dredging and weed cutting undertaken — while in 1956 they showed their commitment to the new found life of canals by opening a hire cruising base at Chester and publishing their first cruising guide — *The Llangollen Canal.*

Under its now accepted new name the canal saw the build up of traffic continue, but had to wait until 1968 before its long term legal position could be clarified. The British Waterways Board had been established in 1963 and over the next five years made one of its priorities to establish the future organisation of its canals. Under the resultant 1968 Transport Act those commercial waterways still undertaking the carriage of goods were identified and listed —while a second list identified the cruising routes, those waterways "to be principally available for cruising, fishing and other recreational purposes". And in this list the Llangollen branch of the old Shropshire Union took its place — rescued from years of disuse and neglect by the unlikely combination of leisure and drinking water — but at last with its future legally assured.

VI : THE WATERWAY TO WALES

At least the name now seems established. The waterway to Wales has seen several changes of title and control over nearly two centuries of life. Constructed as part of the Ellesmere canal system it was to become the Llangollen Branch of the Shropshire Union Canal while also being widely known as the Welsh Canal. But the British Waterways Board notice at the foot of Hurleston Locks expresses no doubt. It is here that one enters the Llangollen Canal.

A good journey should provide a distinct beginning, a middle and an end. The Llangollen offers all of these, its route consisting of three phases — each with its own distinctive character. Turning off the main line of the "Shroppie" the first phase immediately begins — twelve miles during which the canal climbs away from the Cheshire Plain to move into Shropshire and on towards Wales. The ascent begins at once, via the four Hurleston Locks that are overseen by a lock-keeper's cottage and the grass covered walls of the reservoir to the right. Although encountered at the very beginning of the route Hurleston Reservoir was the last major piece of construction work on the canal. In need of more water along the way to Chester — and hence to the Mersey via the Ellesmere Company's separate northern section — it was built between 1835 and 1840. When filled to a depth of some twenty feet it would hold approximately three thousand locks-full of water, the Company reports often translating depth into lockage capacity in this manner. But now with the supply of water for the "Shroppie" main line coming down from Wolverhampton the reservoir is used for the drinking water that has travelled along the route from Wales to be processed here at the adjacent treatment works of the North West Water authority.

Following World War II, when regular navigation of the route got under way again, the early pleasure craft traffic had to contend with deteriorating locks as well as with weed filled pounds between. L.T.C. Rolt, on his 1947 attempt to reach Pontcysyllte was temporarily jammed in an inwardly bulging lock chamber at Baddiley, but the rapid build up of traffic over the following years was to be matched by considerable efforts to improve the condition of the canal. No. 1 Baddiley Lock was, for example, fitted with new mitre gates early in the 1950s. The work force of three carpenters, a blacksmith accompanied by his striker, a sawyer also with his mate and a painter, show how traditional a task the maintenance of canals has remained. Prices have however changed. In 1884 a similar gang would have renewed a pair of mitre gates for around £72 while a single top gate would have cost a mere £32. The documentation of the 1950s shows that the Baddiley mitre gates cost £379 — whereas today such a job would require £9,500 with a single top lock gate replacement needing another £5,000!

The first of the lift bridges, that are such a feature of this route, are soon

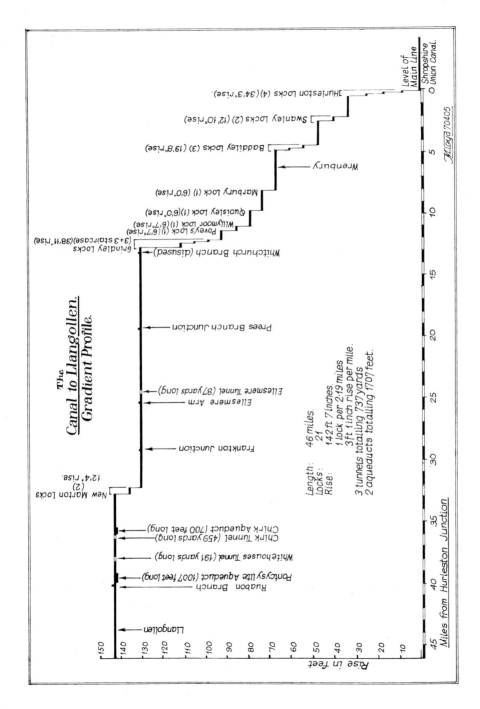

The
Canal to Llangollen.
Gradient Profile.

Length: 46 miles.
Locks: 21
Rise: 142 ft 7 inches
          1 lock per 2.19 miles
          3 ft 1 inch rise per mile
3 tunnels totalling 737 yards
2 aqueducts totalling 1707 feet.

Thurleston Locks (4) (34'3" rise).
Swanley Locks (2) (12'10" rise)
Baddiley Locks (3) (19.8' rise)
Wrenbury
Marbury Lock (1) (6'0" rise)
Quoisley Lock (1) (6'0" rise)
Willeymoor Lock (1) (6'7" rise)
Povey's Lock (1) (6'7" rise)
Grindley Locks (3+3 staircase) (38'11" rise)
Whitchurch Branch (disused)
Prees Branch Junction
Ellesmere Tunnel (87 yards long)
Ellesmere Arm
Frankton Junction
New Marton Locks (2) 12'4" rise.
Chirk Aqueduct (700 feet long)
Chirk Tunnel (459 yards long)
Whitehouses Tunnel (191 yards long)
Pontcysyllte Aqueduct (1007 feet long)
Ruabon Branch
Llangollen

Level of Main Line
Shropshire Union Canal.

Rise in Feet
150 140 130 120 110 100 90 80 70 60 50 40 30 20 10

Miles from Hurleston Junction

Milroy 70405

57

encountered. At Wrenbury an isolated rural example precedes that in the village itself. One by one these single leaf bascule bridges are being replaced. As they are "listed structures" the B.W.B. is required to maintain them so as to preserve their original character. With increases in the weights of road and farm traffic steel is being used to replace wood in their re-construction — while in the interests of safety and ease of use the pivot ends of these bridges are being set back slightly from the canal bank. Their essential features and appearance are however being carefully preserved.

With the old wharf and mills of Wrenbury left behind the gently upward journey continues until — as if with a final impatient rush — the six locks at Grindley Brook lift the canal steeply into Shropshire. Here a cluster of canal side buildings, watched over by the fine bow-fronted lock-keeper's cottage, remind us how this settlement was once busy with commerce where now, in summer, it is thronged with pleasure craft. The first phase of the journey is over and the climb, if not the journey to Wales, is almost complete.

With the Midlands slipping quietly behind the second phase of the route — twenty miles of lockless yet continually varied waterway — now begins: pastureland, peat moss, woodland and lakes all being encountered in turn, with four canal branches and a tunnel thrown in for good measure! The first of these branches was to Whitchurch. From the re-built New Mills lift bridge it is only a short walk up the grassy de-watered canal bed into the town. The branch was abandoned in 1944 and subsequently drained. Despite some tentative plans for restoration it currently remains in a waterless state.

With each mile Wales grows closer until, by Bridge 42 at Tilstock Park, its border with England actually runs along with the towpath for nearly a mile. A roving bridge and red brick canal cottage draw attention back to the waterway as the second of its branches is reached. The Prees branch once ran for nearly four miles, down to limekilns near Quina Brook, but now only the first reedy mile can be used. Here at the navigable limit boats lie in the marina, opened in 1974. This was once a major clay pit, diggers being used to extract the clay which was then boated away for use as a puddling and br' ich mending material for the canal. The Shropshire Union Company used a standard design of horse drawn ice-breaking boat and one of these — the 'Marbury' — lay abandoned in this branch for many years until, in 1972, she was successfully recovered and taken to the Boat Museum at Ellesmere Port for restoration and preservation.

The main line continues west, crossing the peat land of Whixall Moss. Raised on an embankment it traverses a strange and sombre landscape of blacks and browns, bracken and silver birch struggling to grow among the peat cuttings — while on the horizon the hills to come may be glimpsed. But before they are reached the scenery is to change yet again. Gently rolling countryside gives way to woodland and lakes as Ellesmere nears. Between Bridges 53 and 55 the waterway runs above Colemere. In the undergrowth on the bank between canal and lake old boundary posts de-limiting Company property can still be discovered. Those of stone bear the initials EC, the old original Ellesmere Canal, — while short rounded metal posts marked SUC recall the Shropshire Union Company. The delightful combination of lake and woodland continues for a little longer until the canal burrows into the first tunnel of its route; 87 yards underground are to achieve another rapid scene change for on emerging from the darkness the waterway is found to have moved into open parkland with the town of Ellesmere less than a mile ahead.

While Ellesmere saw the initiation of the canal it has also been central to its administration and maintenance. A turn right under Bridge 59 takes one up the stubby arm to the wharf and terminal basin in the town where warehouses and a canal crane still look down on visiting boats — but it is at the junction itself that the hub of the waterway is to be found. In 1805 the Committee "judged it necessary to erect a Canal Office at Ellesmere being the most central point on the Navigation. This will contain a Committee Room, an Office for Accounts and another for Plans ... also apartments connected therewith for the resident Accountant, Agent and the resident Engineer". Beech House, at the junction of the Ellesmere Arm, was the result. The Committee Room, on the ground floor of the bay shaped wing, looks out on the three directions of the waterway, members attending meetings content in the knowledge that the house had been built with extensive wine cellars beneath! Long since converted to flats the "Office" still retains its Georgian elegance while immediately to the west is the more utilitarian Canal Depot built at the same time.

It is from these buildings that B.W.B. continue to maintain the canal —but although still busy it sees far less activity than in the heyday of the Shropshire Union. Almost everything needed by a waterway has been made or repaired at the Depot at some time or another. For many years lock gates for the whole S.U. system as well as for farther afield were built here. Gates for the Trent & Mersey and for the Leeds & Liverpool canals have also been made at Ellesmere before being boated away to their destinations. Much of the oak and other woods originally used in gate construction was grown locally, the S.U. Company owning its own woodlands as well as buying in from the Bridgewater Estate whose timber yard was situated at the head of the Ellesmere arm. Boats have also been built, converted and repaired here — the dry dock remaining in use today.

From cranes to filing cabinets, from sheds to office desks — all have been made at Ellesmere for use on the S.U. system. The workshops still house a marvellous collection of patterns, casts and templates as needed to make such items as tow path rails, mile posts and lock gate fittings. The works yard once boasted a massive travelling overhead crane but, while this has long since been demolished, the buildings still contain the belts and pulleys that once drove saws and blacksmith's bellows. Power originally came from an old Cornish steam engine but this was later replaced by another steam engine assembled from modified locomotive parts obtained from the Crewe railway works. As befits a railway controlled canal the Company did not forget its cats. To support them in their mice catching duties — as with railway stations — the Depot also received a small feeding allowance for its feline helpers. The interior doors of the Depot still retain the cat holes that allowed them to wander through the buildings in search of their prey!

Mr. Jack Strange spent his long working life based on the Depot — starting in 1938 as a lad of 16½ years old and employed to help in the blacksmith's shop. He was to retire nearly half a century later from the post of Section Foreman with a wealth of memories of life on the canal. During the quiet years that followed the ending of commercial traffic on the waterway only a few maintenance boats travelled its lengths. Well known among these was the boat 'Antwerp' almost always in charge of Mr. Jack Roberts and his horse 'Molly'. Jack Strange tells of the trials of a blacksmith's life. Having just completed re-shoeing a horse for Jack Roberts the railway company vet arrived for one of his regular inspections of livestock. Listening to the horse's heart he announced it totally unfit for work and liable to drop dead at any moment. The unfortunate animal — a new shoe shining on each of its hooves — was immediately put down!

Winding on through the rich dairying pastures of Shropshire the canal then reaches the most significant junction of its route — that at Welsh Frankton. From here the old line to Llanymynech, Welshpool and Newtown went south. The bridge numbering system that started at Hurleston, 29 miles away, continues south towards Newtown — this route being considered the main line in carrying days. Accordingly bridge numbering starts afresh as the canal to Llangollen moves away west. Abandoned since the breach of 1936 hopes for its complete restoration of the southern route are now high. The four Frankton locks were re-opened in the Autumn of 1987 while a Bill to restore the 'Montgomery Canal' to full navigation as part of the cruising waterways network was passed through Parliament in December of the same year. The Llangollen route, now moving almost due west, completes its climb via the two remote New Marton locks and moves on towards Chirk. As the land grows hillier the third and final phase of the journey to Wales is about to begin.

The last ten miles of the canal to Llangollen provide enormous variety. In quick succession the landscape changes from the pastoral to the industrial then back to the deeply rural as the waterway completes its journey up the steep sided valley of the Dee into the hills. Although lockless this final section contains some of the most spectacular and important canal engineering structures within the land. Entering the Ceiriog valley, in company with the busy A5 road, the waterway soon reaches the first of these. The Chirk Aqueduct carries boats high above the tumbling river and provides a dramatic entry into Wales. Alongside stands the taller railway viaduct of 1848 but since its opening in 1801 the older Chirk Aqueduct has remained a masterpiece of canal engineering. Immediately the canal dives into Chirk Tunnel. Spacious and bricklined, boatmen must have been grateful that Telford had provided this and the other tunnels on the route with towpaths — some of the first to include such and which eliminated the tiresome and inhuman practice of "legging". Having passed Chirk Cutting, plagued with slips over many years and recently enlarged, a winding hole marks the former entrance to Black Park Basin. 191 damp and dripping yards take one through Whitehouses Tunnel and on emerging into the open the canal hugs the hillside to swing west into the Vale of Llangollen.

Across the river the industrial sprawl begins — the chimneys of Monsanto Chemicals rising above the site where once the Plas Kynaston foundry cast the iron for the canal's two aqueducts. Once under the lift bridge at Fron the canal swings right onto a huge embankment. Tree lined, this resembles a triumphant avenue and leads to Pontcysyllte Aqueduct itself. Although built before the railway age and larger feats of civil engineering it remains a breathtaking experience to take a boat through the narrow iron trough that leaps 1007 feet across the River Dee.

Trevor Basin, once busy with iron, coal, chemicals and pottery traffic, is now thronged with pleasure craft. Two interesting old buildings survive: Scotch Hall, an impressive white house believed to have been used by Telford during the canal's construction and a smaller stone cottage; the Old Accounts Office, the former pay office for the navvies who built the canal. Ignoring the short length of the abandoned Ruabon Arm ahead the route to Llangollen involves a tight turn left into the narrow water feeder line. Within a mile the canal is cradled in the hills as it winds its way to its destination. To the right lie the huge limestone cliffs from where stone was once brought down by tramway to be loaded onto boats at Bridge 41, while to the left and below the River Dee tumbles its way back to Pontcysyllte. The final mile into Llangollen is among the loveliest on the route. Hill, pasture, tree and canal achieve a natural unity as the waterway passes under the last lift bridge and onto the rocky shelf that carries it finally into the slate roofed town.

Canal wharf and warehouse perch inconveniently high above the settlement that once they served. The permanent Canal Exhibition Centre located here reminds of the past commercial uses of this waterway. Now busy with day visitors, hire craft and the horse drawn trip boats that have operated from here for over a century, the site continues to serve a very real purpose. Only $1\frac{1}{2}$ miles remain — up the narrow yet navigable feeder that supplies water from the River Dee to the rest of the route as well as to the taps of Cheshire. After the final winding hole the suburban fringe of Llangollen starts to thin until by Bridge 46 open country is reached again. Here, immediately to the south of the canal, the International Music Eisteddfod is held every July. Also to the south the Dee tumbles past on its rocky route — parallel to it the old Great Western Railway line to Corwen. Two miles of the track from Llangollen have now been restored so that steam trains can once again run to the attractively re-built Berwyn station that clings to the hillside above the river.

A final curve and the end of the canal is in sight. Here water enters the feeder from the weir known as Horseshoe Falls. In a large stone built semi-circle this curves across the river to sluices on the northern bank. Through these water is passed to the canal. From the time that the water-line was opened in 1808 it did so unchecked, but since the 1944 Act of Parliament the flow has been carefully metered, via the equipment housed in the brick built gauging house. Ahead of the millions of gallons that pass each day lie the 46 miles to Hurleston and beyond.

When in April 1921 the walls of Hurleston No. 3 lock "moved bodily inwards 14 inches" the engineer's report pointed out that it had after all "been built upwards of 120 years ago". Such durability cannot be taken for granted for the banks and bridges, tunnels, locks, aqueducts and culverts of the waterway all require regular inspection and maintenance. Paradoxically the

The consequence of the major canal breach that took place west of Trevor on 7th September 1945. The waterway — above and to the right — burst its banks to wash away some 120 feet of railway embankment. The goods train, seen here, plunged into the gap to completely burn out. The driver was killed but, though injured, the fireman and guard escaped.

major structures of the Llangollen have caused relatively little concern —albeit cracks and fractures found in the Pontcysyllte aqueduct have caused some temporary closures since World War II. Instead it is the unglamorous yet crucial banks and canal bed that have caused the major problems and expense.

The complex geology of the area with its unstable mix of strata is mainly to blame. The breaches of 1917 and 1936 were to cause the closure of the Weston and Llanymynech branches but it is further west from Chirk onwards that the major problems of recent years have occurred. The traditional method of dealing with small breaches is to fill the gaps with stones, pack them with wet sand and complete the repair with a layer of puddled clay. But when a major burst occurs more drastic measures are called for as the recent history of these upper reaches of the canal has clearly shown.

The water line, west of Trevor, is built on particularly unstable ground. In the early hours of September 7th, 1945 a massive breach in the vicinity of Sun Trevor Inn de-watered the canal. Some 2 million gallons cascaded down, sweeping away 120 feet of the railway embankment below. The rails remained suspended in the air. Shortly after 4.00 a.m. a goods train set out for Llangollen along the darkened route. Plunging into the sizeable gap in the track bed it burst into flames. The driver was killed outright but the guard and fireman miraculously escaped with their lives.

Breaches and closures have gone on ever since. A major burst in 1960 was to be followed by a stoppage for repairs along the whole Trevor to Llangollen section in the summer of 1978. Four years later much of this work was to be swept away when a 50 yard breach occurred west of Bridge 35. Obviously drastic measured were needed — as confirmed early in 1985 when yet another serious slippage tore away some of the more recent repairs. A complete survey, inclusive of geological bore holes, has since been undertaken and has established that traditional repairs to the canal are simply not enough. Without the construction of strong water retaining structures resting on a sound well drained base further slippages to a route that clings to the sides of the steep sided valley of the Dee are inevitable. The old puddled clay bed of the feeder — in some places merely resting on a loose backfill of shale and brushwood — has reached the end of its useful days.

A total re-instatement of the route is now underway. Whole lengths of the canal are being re-laid in a sectioned concrete trough. Each reinforced $7\frac{1}{2}$ metre length unit forms a separate watertight unit which, when joined to its neighbours, makes up the new channel. This rests on a well-drained backfill and a waterproof membrane so as to ensure that problems of water erosion from beneath can no longer occur. For the twenty two winter weeks of each year, under the direction of B.W.B. engineers, teams of contractors will continue to work on the various stages of the scheme — the highest risk sections being tackled first. Eventually much of the canal between Gledrid and Llangollen will have been re-built in this way.

Where horse drawn slate boats once used the narrow feeder above Llangollen horse drawn pleasure craft have also traded for over a century. The first trip boats appeared on the canal in 1884. In the early years Captain Jones held the concession from the Shropshire Union company on payment of an annual rent. Obviously he had some marketing flair for a contemporary postcard of the pre-World War I scene was to bear the message that "pleasure boats run up and down this canal, the Welsh people on board singing their sweet choruses"! The concession then passed to a Mr. Isaac Roberts whose annual rent was reduced from £150 per annum to £120 during the First World War "due to the traffic's decline consequent upon hostilities". Immediately after the Second World War his successor — a Mr. A. Roberts — also had cause to grumble, but in his case as to the poor condition of the canal and the growing competition he now faced from motor coaches. But there is no doubt as to the popularity and levels of pleasure traffic today. Trip boats of various types have operated over the years. These have ranged from early Sunday School outings, and in contrast to trips for thirsty Welshman travelling over the Chirk aqueduct into England — where the pubs stayed open on Sundays!

At the manned locks on the route — New Marton, Grindley Brook and Hurleston — meters record the rate of water flow and hence the number of boats that pass may be calculated. Since the pioneering days of the 1950s pleasure traffic has steadily built up so that today well over 300 boats may be moving along the Llangollen within a busy summer's week, making it the most popular of all our cruising waterways. With a continuing investment in its maintenance and in the re-instatement of its upper lengths the British Waterways Board have demonstrated their faith in its future — while all who pass along the infinitely varied and delightful lengths of this canal can have little doubt as to the unique and continued attractions of this waterway to Wales.

New beginnings — early 1987 and part of the major re-instatement programme undertaken by British Waterways Board to protect the canal from further breaches on its troubled western end. A section of re-inforced concrete trough is being cast on site, lengths of such channelling being joined together to form a virtually new waterway along the existing route.